THE ROAD TO ZERO

IVÁN DUQUE

THE ROAD TO ZERO
Colombia's strategy for carbon neutrality

Work edited in collaboration with Editorial Planeta – Colombia

Original title: *El camino a cero*

Translated from the Spanish by Azzam Alkadhi

© 2021, Iván Duque

© 2021, Editorial Planeta Colombiana S. A. – Bogotá, Colombia

Derechos reservados

© 2022, Editorial Planeta Mexicana, S.A. de C.V.
Bajo el sello editorial PLANETA M.R.
Avenida Presidente Masarik núm. 111,
Piso 2, Polanco V Sección, Miguel Hidalgo
C.P. 11560, Ciudad de México
www.planetadelibros.com.mx
www.paidos.com.mx

Cover design: Grupo Planeta Art Department

Insert photos:
© Ministry of Environment and Sustainable Development
© Nicolás Galeano
© Juan Pablo Bello

First edition printed in English in Colombia: April 2022
ISBN: 978-958-42-9837-9

First edition printed in English in México: April 2022
ISBN: 978-607-07-8839-0

This book was printed in Impresora Tauro, S.A. de C.V.
Año de Juárez Av. No. 343, Granjas San Antonio,
Iztapalapa, C.P. 09070, Mexico City
Printed and made in Mexico / *Impreso y hecho en México*

To all those Colombians who dedicate their lives to protecting the environment and building a carbon neutral society.

What kind of world do we want to leave for those who come after us? What is at stake is our own dignity. Leaving an inhabitable planet to future generations is, first and foremost, up to us.

POPE FRANCIS

CONTENTS

ACKNOWLEDGEMENTS

This book was made possible by the many people who have joined me and backed me in my goal of building an environmental plan for Colombia, which will allow us to achieve carbon neutrality by 2050 and a 51% reduction in our greenhouse gas (GHG) emissions by the year 2030.

I would like to thank María Paula Correa, Víctor Muñoz, Carlos Eduardo Correa, Diego Mesa, Rodolfo Zea, Daniel Palacios, Diego Molano, Francisco Cruz, Nicolás Galarza, Alejandro Salas, Melissa Mora, Hassan Nassar, Soraya Yanine, Carlos Cortés, Cristian Samper, Juan Pablo Bonilla, Sergio Diazgranados, Ángela Orozco, Luis Guillermo Echeverri, Felipe Bayón, Fabio Arjona, Hernando García, Klaus Schwab, Mauricio Claver, Bernardo Álvarez, Enric Sala, Orlando Molano, Tom Lovejoy, Carter Roberts, Andrew Steer, Henry Paulson, Howard Buffet, Jeff Bezos, Frank Mars, Alexandra Moreira, Juan Carlos Pinzón, Ricardo Lozano and Yolanda González. I would equally like to thank President

Sebastián Piñera of Chile, Costa Rica's President Carlos Alvarado and President Emmanuel Macron of France; Prime Minister Boris Johnson of the United Kingdom; and John Kerry, US Special Presidential Envoy for Climate. Thanks also to COP26 leader, Alok Sharma, the United Kingdom's Minister for the Pacific and International Environment, Zac Goldsmith, and vice-president of Colombia, Martha Lucía Ramírez, for the conversations and support they have given me in dealing with the challenges posed for a country like Colombia by climate change, and choosing the most suitable course of action. Thanks to Juanita Escallón for her valuable contributions and impeccable editing of this book and to Grupo Planeta for publishing it. Finally, and with my whole heart, I thank my wife María Juliana, who always enriches my thoughts with her opinions and comments; thanks to Luciana, Matías and Eloísa, the driving force in my life, and to my brother Andrés, my partner and confidant.

W herever we come from, whatever we believe, we all share this one small planet – and if we don't all start pulling in the same direction, we will all eventually feel the effects of its changing climate.

That's why I've long been such a passionate advocate for international action on climate change, and it's why I'm delighted to see President Duque setting out such a positive vision for Colombia's net zero future. It's one none of us should be afraid to embrace. Because as this book shows, doing the right thing by our environment and our planet does not have to mean sacrificing jobs or living standards.

A dozen or more years hence, drivers in Colombia and the UK will still roam far and wide in their cars – but they will do so in electric vehicles rather than choking the air with dirty old fossil fuels. Aircraft will still soar between El Dorado and Heathrow – but they will be the clean, efficient "jet zero" planes of the future. When our children or grandchildren flick a switch on the wall, the lights will still come on – powered not by coal or oil or gas, but by energy snatched from the wind or sun or seas. And when they venture out into the world of work, they won't find a landscape decimated by the loss of old, polluting industries, but one filled with the opportunities of the new.

Any kind of change to the way we live our lives can bring with it a degree of trepidation. It takes real courage for leaders to stand up to entrenched interests and age-old attitudes and take their people and their country in a bold new direction. But as President Duque sets out here, we are running out of time to act on climate change. We simply must take the concrete steps needed to keep global temperature change below 1.5 °c. And we need every country in the world to play its part.

The strategy set out in this book puts Colombia at the leading edge of the race to net zero. I wish the people of Colombia every success in implementing it, and setting a much-needed example for the world to follow.

BORIS JOHNSON
Primer ministro del Reino Unido

The road to zero is possible

We live in a world rife with challenges to humanity's existence. Without doubt, the greatest is the climate crisis we have caused over many centuries and which, today, demands the most radical conditions from us as a species in our time on this planet. Dealing with the climate crisis calls for ethics, morality, conscientiousness, creativity, intelligence, solidarity, innovation and knowledge management. These characteristics, unique to our species, are what we need in order to save the planet and leave behind a better future for generations to come.

The way we act starts with recognizing that, each year on this planet, we are producing almost 51 billion tons of greenhouse gases (GHG) and that these, in turn, are leading to dangerous increases in global warming, up to the point of contributing to a rise in sea levels, the melting of ice caps and snow-capped mountains and a rise in temperatures which brings about the arrival of transmissible diseases. All of this combined leads to a rise in the tragic consequences of natural disasters.

Recognizing this harsh reality means understanding that, for centuries, the development agenda did not take into account the effects of CO_2 and GHG emissions and that we were intent on "progressing" with industries and a form of consumption which ignored the devastating effects they created for humanity. Many people will say that we have recognized our mistake and will point to almost two decades of a proliferation of conferences, forums, declarations, treaties and political actions, but the truth is that, beyond the good intentions and actions carried out in good faith, we find ourselves reaching a point of no return, and if we do not act decisively, the irreversible damage will destroy humanity.

The reality that I am sharing should motivate us to make clear goals and to recognize that all of our actions and means of working and co-existing as humans lead to GHG emissions. That is why the path is not a road to zero emissions, but instead to being able to neutralize emissions with our behavior and creative capacity as soon as possible. Similarly, as we attempt to neutralize emissions, it is always necessary to forge a path towards the conservation and protection of nature, something we could call a carbon neutral-nature positive path.

How quickly do we need to act? There is no time to lose; we have to act right now and quicker than ever. In order to do that, there are two dates we cannot ignore: 2030 and 2050. By 2030, we need to achieve the greatest GHG emission reductions in history, and by 2050 we need to ensure that the greatest number of countries possible are carbon neutral and nature positive. Today, these goals are part of our raison d'être, and meeting them means making progress in energy transition, cleaner transportation, establishing a circular economy, stopping deforestation and planting trees en masse, extending protected areas, changing production and consumption habits, and involving indigenous communities in nature-based solutions. It also means building a new generation of green businesses, where payments for environmental services are a new way of life, where we protect the Amazon, all of the planet's forests and high mountain ecosystems (also known as paramos), and where we implement the most intelligent waste management system in our history. Of course, we also need a new 21st century set of ethics, where our individual behavior aims to reduce the carbon footprint of all of our activities.

What is the role of Colombia and Colombians in this setting? Colombia represents just 0.6% of global GHG emissions, but it is one of the most vulnerable countries to the devastating effects of climate change. Furthermore, our beautiful country is the second-most biodiverse in the world, and is home to 52% of existing paramos. The way Colombia acts is, therefore, an example, an important call for global action and, above all, a call to the richest and most powerful nations to realize that, if Colombia can do it, they too should follow the same path.

The targets we have proposed are conclusive and call for a large national pact in order to meet them. Colombia has proposed a reduction of 51% in its GHG emissions by 2030, and the attainment of carbon neutrality by 2050. Similarly, we have committed to zero deforestation by 2030 and, by the same year, if not before, having 30% of our territory in protected areas. They are ambitious, but attainable goals, requiring the clear interaction of all sectors in this existential purpose.

Reaching this objective is far removed from the sterile political debates and polarization which trouble all the countries of the world. Doing the right thing and meeting our goals is not about being left or right, it does not belong to any party, is not aimed at any electoral purpose, it is simply our duty and we must all contribute. By speeding up the implementation of more non-conventional, renewable energy sources, we are making big strides; by increasing our automobile fleet with more electric or hybrid vehicles, we are contributing to a more eco-friendly transportation model; by defeating deforestation and planting trees on a massive, permanent scale, we are capturing emissions and protecting flora and fauna; by making Colombia a regional model of circular economy, we are creating a new collective ethos.

The goals that Colombia has taken on as part of Glasgow's COP26 and Biological Diversity COP15 are part of the vision of a country which has in its biodiversity its greatest riches and greatest distinction on the international stage. Colombia wants to be an example, but at the same time it wants to propose real and practical solutions for gaining access to funding and resources which allow us to speed up the outlined goals and meet them while generating well-being, employment and growth.

This book is the product of my reflections on life and long work days over many years. It is my way of condensing concepts, principles, values and convictions that have always been with me. It is also the product of the daily efforts of a government with numerous collaborators, scientists, businesspeople, activists and citizens aiming to define our national environmental roadmap and achieve unquestionable results which can then become state policies and the continuous commitment of multiple actors.

These pages have been cultivated with my participation in numerous forums and spaces, in public policies and regulations, but most importantly they have come from my daily reflections and notes which I constantly take on my responsibilities as president of Colombia. This is not a political book, but a space for sharing a purpose for our nation, in which we can all participate and contribute enthusiastically.

The environmental cause has been my life's cause. As a child, my parents took me to the Amazon, to Chingaza to see the paramos, to the swamplands, to Colombia's rivers, to the snow-capped peaks. Above all, they taught me the value of respecting, loving and defending the natural riches which surround us. In all of my public and private responsibilities, I have taken paths and actions to contribute to this conviction, and in all the academic training and teaching spaces, I have proposed this agenda in order to spur myself on. This book is, therefore, a humble contribution to collective construction, to immediate action and to humanity's transformation.

The road to zero is the path to zero net emissions[1] which will result from achieving carbon neutrality and the positive natural conservation that we are proposing. These pages will outline what we have achieved and what we must achieve so that Colombia can contribute to the protection of our shared home. So, I invite you to join me on the ROAD TO ZERO. Together we will get there.

BOGOTA, 27 SEPTEMBER, 2021

---

1   Hereinafter, all references to *zero emissions* will be understood as *zero net emissions*.

CHAPTER 1

Colombia, committed to the environment

B ill Gates begins his book, *How to Avoid a Climate Disaster*, with the following phrase: "There are two numbers you need to know about climate change. The first is 51 billion. The other is zero". Gates is right.

Fifty-one billion is the number of tons of gases that the world emits and which reach our atmosphere each year, causing what is known as the *greenhouse effect*. The bad news is that this number increases each year, so the figure only refers to the current situation. Zero is the ideal number we need to reach: if we want to halt global warming and not live through the terrible effects that scientists have warned us about in recent years, our mission should be to lower the number from 51 billion tons to zero tons as soon as possible.

It sounds like mission impossible, and it certainly is a difficult task. It is everyone's responsibility: you, the readers, can start at home with your daily routines, while governments and their representatives have the duty to change the way we do things. In Colombia, we have already started to take measures in this regard, and I am proud to say that we are a country committed to halting climate change, to biodiversity and to improving our practices so that our planet can breathe more easily and future generations can enjoy their lives. If we do not act fast, in the 2030s, Earth will be 1.5 degrees Celsius warmer, according to a report by the United Nations Intergovernmental Panel on Climate Change (IPCC)[2].

Faced with this panorama, and taking on the responsibility that we have as human beings, it is time to ask ourselves: what are we prepared to do to reduce GHG production on a large scale and stop the devastating outcome which, as things stand, it looks as though we will be faced with? In the words of Bill Gates, how are we going to get to zero?

Humanity faces a race against time, perhaps the most important one in our lifetime and that of future generations. Are we ready?

Our responsibility to biodiversity

"Produce while preserving, and preserve while producing" is the commitment we as the Colombian state made in order to mitigate the impact of climate change. It is a fact that we are facing the greatest environmental threat that we have seen, which could have irreversible effects due to a change in climate, a direct and indirect result of

2   See: https://www.bbc.com/mundo/noticias-45785972.

human activity. Therefore, in line with the various cross-cutting state policies adopted by different countries, Colombia signed a Sustainability Pact in 2018, with the aim of safeguarding natural resources for future generations. To do this it is vital to strike a balance between the conservation of the environment, the responsible use of the environment and the development of national production. The natural riches of our territory are strategic assets for the nation, which is why it is essential to conserve biodiversity, through sustainable use and the development of responsible economic production alternatives.

In order to reach this goal, the pact has a cross-cutting nature: all entities (public and private), ministries, regions, municipalities, international entities and civil society must work together and in an organized fashion in order to preserve the environment, reduce carbon dioxide emissions, which we already know need to reach zero, and deal with climate change. While on this path, it is vital to counteract deforestation and the illegal trade of flora and fauna, as well as other dynamics which contribute to the degradation of ecosystems.

Concerned about the environment, the younger generations have mobilized and brought about an environmental revolution which we should all join. Young people understand that real change is in our hands and it is up to us, as human beings, to transform the climactic reality we are facing today. Which is why they are so persistent when it comes to the need for civic culture to keep transforming, constantly giving more priority to practices such as recycling, being more conscientious with their purchases - clothes shopping, for example – and cultivating habits (such as switching off lights that they are not using) in order to make responsible use of environmental resources.

The Colombian state wants to support younger generations so that all of these actions have an impact on the environment, which is why the idea of "Produce while preserving, and preserve while producing" is so key. But what does this strategy and commitment involve? In general terms, achieving an efficient use of natural resources, raw materials and energy.

Taking care of the planet and preventing a climactic disaster are not simply trending topics. They require everyone's commitment, and it is therefore key to understand that the environment is a cross-cutting factor in local and national government plans, in private sector company guidelines and in the everyday actions of all human beings. Therefore, different circular economy blueprints, science-based schemes, innovation and the adoption of new technologies all come into play as part of this strategy.

It is clear that the economy is an essential element of any action plan related to the environment. Consequently, it is vital that all entities work together to implement strategies that manage activities and processes that have a negative impact on the environment. We need new instruments and developments which allow us to drive sustainable innovation.

Natural resources are national treasures, so when it comes to conserving biodiversity, the entire state machinery should be geared towards control actions in territories where there is the greatest concentration of threats to the environment, as well as promoting new economic opportunities, locally. This way, we can meet objectives such as reducing tree and forest felling resulting from the disorganized expansion of the agricultural frontier, combating land-grabbing, and strengthening territorial control of illicit activities related to mineral exploitation, the extraction of forest resources and crops. We can also promote inclusive production alternatives and opportunities, generate and strengthen alliances between the public-private sectors, international partners and civil society, and create strategies for the productive transformation of sectors.

Furthermore, for the Conservation Pact to be sustainable over time, it is crucial for there to be a joint effort between the ministries, other government entities and the countries in the region which have a direct impact on Colombia's environmental development. Strategies must be focused on prevention and reduction of disaster risks, and reducing negative impacts on the environment.

All of this will be possible if we promote working with the communities by disseminating knowledge and information, such that they can make better decisions regarding disaster risks and the effects of climate change. Similarly, it is vital to strengthen environmental institutions and promote optimal investigation and public management, in order to foster dialogue within the territories and guarantee environmental education.

Colombia's environmental challenges

The Sustainability Pact signed in Colombia is directly related to the Sustainable Development Goals (SDGs). The path to 2030 implies a commitment that is more than just a piece of paper: the country must guarantee a modern environmental plan, in which the generation of new earning opportunities and the conservation of biodiversity are prioritized.

The commitment, therefore, is to promote environmental management in order to mitigate climate change through the strengthening of territories in the face of disasters and risks, the construction of processes and provision of appropriate information. In this sense, production sectors, the private sector, academia and the general public can contribute to social transformation, through education, an environmental culture, and dialogue and conflict management relating to landgrabbing.

Specifically, the actions promoted via the pact will contribute to the agricultural, transport, energy, industrial and housing sectors being able to convert their production processes into sustainable ones. Thus, it will be possible to:

1. Reduce greenhouse gas (GHG) emissions, such that Colombia can meet the 2030 Paris Agreement commitments.

2. Increase recycling, reuse of water and energy efficiency, through a national circular economy strategy which will reduce the intensity of material usage.

3. Adopt protocols so that state entities can coordinate immediate actions to protect the environment, with the support of the National Council for the Fight Against Environmental Crimes.

4. Prioritize the restoration of ecosystems using various incentives, such as economic signals from the state, in order to reduce air contamination and promote better treatment of residual water.

5. Implement initiatives with accessible, transparent and efficient information, in order to reduce the effects of droughts, floods and natural phenomena.

6. Make recommendations so that the granting of environmental licenses, the standardization of pro-

cedures and other environmental control instruments are effective.

7. Strengthen regional environmental authorities in order to optimize environmental management, surveillance and civic service.

The commitments of the ministries

With the "Produce while preserving, and preserve while producing" strategy, every sector contributes, and comprehensive state intervention guarantees: progress in the transition to production activities which are committed to the mitigation of climate change; an improvement in air, water and soil quality, thus preventing impacts on public health and reducing inequality in access to resources; an acceleration in the circular economy, and the development of new financial, economic and market instruments which drive sustainable activities.

With this in mind, the government has proposed clear goals in order to comply with the Sustainability Pact, as we want to set an example for our citizens and the world. Consequently, each ministry is committed to one or two specific tasks related to its sector, with the aim of making progress in meeting the following four objectives:

- **Objective 1.** Progressing in the transition to production activities which are committed to sustainability and the mitigation of climate change.

- **Objective 2.** Improving air, water and soil quality, thus preventing impacts on public health and reducing inequality in access to resources.

- **Objective 3.** Speeding up the circular economy as the basis for waste reduction, reuse and recycling.

- **Objective 4.** Developing new financial, economic and market instruments in order to drive activities committed to sustainability and the mitigation of climate change.

In the following table, I outline the specific tasks of each ministry, by area, in order to meet the four objectives.

As you have read so far, caring for our environment is an enormous challenge that we must all take on. Modifying our routines and the way we produce and consume will not be an easy task, nor will achieving the goal of zero GHG emissions.

TABLE 1. THE TASKS OF EACH MINISTRY IN ORDER TO MEET OBJECTIVES

OBJECTIVE 1.
Progressing in the transition to production activities which are committed to sustainability and the mitigation of climate change

AREA	SPECIFIC TASKS
Agricultural production with sustainable practices	• The Ministries of Agriculture, and the Environment and Sustainable Development will promote sustainable agricultural production. They must therefore develop a strategy to convert agricultural, fishing and livestock production systems into sustainable, climate-intelligent models with better techniques and technology. • The Ministry of Agriculture should define a methodology which prioritizes projects for land adaptation, the comprehensive management of water resources, the use of efficient technologies and planning based on hydrometeorological information and climate change risks.
Sustainable transport	• The Ministry of Transport, with the support of the Ministries of the Environment, Mining and the Treasury, and the Mining and Energy Planning Unit (UPME, for its Spanish acronym), will implement a strategy which promotes sustainable transport, whether it be by road, rail, waterways or air. The objective is to increase the ingress of clean vehicles and reduce import duties. • The Ministry of Transport will adjust programs of decommissioning and renovation of public bus fleets and trucks. • The Ministry of Transport will promote sustainable urban transportation with the implementation of Nationally-Appropriated Mitigation Actions (NAMA) in order to reduce journeys and prioritize non-motorized means of transport, including bicycles.
Conventional non-renewable energy and energy efficiency	• The Ministry of Mining will establish guidelines for incorporating energy storage systems in the electric system.

38

AREA	SPECIFIC TASKS
Conventional non-renewable energy and energy efficiency	• The Ministry of Mining, with the support of UPME, will promote the roll out of the advanced measuring infrastructure, including: evaluating the potential to develop district heating plants; updating regulations and frameworks for energy labelling; evaluating a blueprint for real-time hourly rates and new business models for electricity retail sales, in order to increase the country's energy efficiency.
Technological conversion for sustainable, low-carbon industry	• The Ministry of Environment, with the support of the Ministry of Information Technology and Communication, will update environmental guides in order to strengthen industrial environmental management and performance. Portfolios will be developed with good environmental techniques and practices in prioritized sectors, in order to contribute to improving air quality. • The Ministry of Information Technology and Communication, with the support of the Ministry of Environment, will implement a strategy to develop conversion projects and technological innovation in industries with environmental, technical and financial viability. • The Ministry of Information Technology and Communication, with the support of UPME and the Ministry of Mining, will implement an inter-institutional strategy for energy management in the industrial sector which contributes to a reduction in GHG emissions.
Sustainable construction and infrastructure	• The Ministry of Housing will develop a tool for quantifying losses in the water system. Thus, it will promote the development of a sustainable drinking water and sewage infrastructure. It will also formulate guidelines for the application of sustainable urban drainage systems in regions with a water shortage, and implement a national strategy in cities with projects for the mitigation of and adaptation to climate change.

OBJECTIVE 2.
Improving air, water and soil quality, thus preventing impacts on public health and reducing inequality in access to resources

AREA	SPECIFIC TASKS
Improving air quality in order to protect public health	• The Ministry of Environment will update the emission standards of mobile sources in order to meet EURO VI standards. In partnership with the Ministry of Mining, it will regulate the sulfur content in fuel in order to reduce atmospheric contamination in Colombia. • The Ministry of Environment will establish the national program for the substitution of wood-burning stoves with efficient stoves. • The Ministry of Environment, with the Institute of Hydrology, Meteorology and Environmental Studies (IDEAM, for its Spanish acronym), will implement a program to improve the coverage and availability of information on emissions and air quality. It will also support environmental authorities in strengthening the control and surveillance of emissions with strategic actions and mechanisms for civilian participation.
Reducing pressure on and improving the quality of water resources	• The Ministry of Environment will promote the implementation of the National Hydrological Plan, particularly focused on programs for hydrological regulation, subterranean waters, legalizing users, and water investigation and monitoring. • The Ministry of Housing will optimize the treatment of municipal waste, incorporating guidelines for new technologies and regulating regional services, through vertical, superficial, subterranean and marine disintegration.
Managing environmental and soil liabilities	• The Ministry of Environment, with the support of the Ministries of Mining, Housing, Information Technology and Agriculture, will implement the program for managing environmental liabilities. • The Ministry of Environment, with the support of the Ministry of Agriculture, IDEAM, the Rural Agricultural Planning Unit (UPRA, for its Spanish acronym), and the Agustin Codazzi Geographical Institute (IGAC, for its Spanish acronym), will study the physical and chemical state of the soil. • The Ministries of the Environment, Health, Labor, and Information Technology and Communication will implement the program for managing industrial chemical substances.

AREA	SPECIFIC TASKS
Managing chemical substances and hazardous waste	• The Labor Ministry, alongside the Ministries of Health and Housing, and the National Unit for Disaster Risk Management (UNGRD, for its Spanish acronym), will implement the program for preventing major accidents. • The Ministries of the Environment, Mining, Information Technology and Communication, Health, and Defense will strengthen strategies for eliminating the use of mercury and other substances which affect public health and the environment.

OBJECTIVE 3.
Speeding up the circular economy as the basis for waste reduction, reuse and recycling

AREA	SPECIFIC TASKS
Promoting a circular economy in production processes	• The Ministries of Information Technology and Communication, and the Environment will define the national circular economy strategy aimed at the industrial sector, in order for it to incorporate eco-design, eco-innovation and industrial symbiosis in its processes. • The Administrative Department of Science, Technology and Innovation (Colciencias), with the support of the Ministries of Information Technology and Communications, and the Environment, will develop investigation projects on the potential productive uses of materials which are difficult to exploit. • The Ministry of Environment will establish a mechanism for improving the coverage and effectiveness of ecolabels and the Colombian Environmental Seal for international positioning. • The Ministry of Environment will modify the regulations on the reuse of treated water, based on technical criteria and information provided by various sectors. • The Ministry of Environment will evaluate the effectiveness of extended producer responsibility programs which have been running for more than five years; inclusion of new waste streams and mechanisms for monitoring the management of this waste.

Continues on the next page

AREA	SPECIFIC TASKS
Promoting a circular economy in production processes	• The Ministry of Environment will implement a strategy for promoting the circular economy of plastic streams and other single-use materials in coastal and inland areas, and develop a post-use program for packaging and containers.
Increasing the use, recycling and treatment of waste	• The Ministry of Housing, with the support of the Ministry of Environment, will define criteria for the material recovery infrastructure, fostering the use, recycling and treatment of waste. • The Ministry of Housing will establish the guidelines for the Technical Regulations for the Drinking Water and Basic Sanitation Sector (RAS, for its Spanish acronym), in terms of the use of biosolids and biogases generated by the treatment of municipal sewage. • The Ministry of Housing will adjust the Colombian regulations on earthquake-resistant constructions so that the use of concrete aggregates and aggregate stone in the construction of infrastructure is viable.

OBJECTIVE 4.
Developing new financial, economic and market instruments in order to drive activities committed to sustainability and the mitigation of climate change

AREA	SPECIFIC TASKS
Financial instruments for stimulating the production sector in its transition to sustainability	• The Ministry of Mining will establish the guidelines for agents of the energy services sector to participate in the energy efficiency market. • The National Planning Department (DNP, for its Spanish acronym), with the support of the Ministries of Environment and Housing, will develop the methodology for tracking investments in climate change, including green bonds and other economic instruments.

AREA	SPECIFIC TASKS
Funding for the mitigation of climate change	• The Ministries of Housing and the Environment, and the DNP, will implement a climate funding strategy, which includes new financial frameworks, and fiscal, non-fiscal and market instruments for the reduction of GHG emissions and the efficient use of resources in all production sectors. • The Ministry of Environment, with the support of the DNP and IDEAM, will design the national program for tradable GHG emissions permits, in line with existing economic instruments, such as the carbon tax.
Environmental taxes	• The Ministry of Environment, with the support of the Ministries of Housing, Agriculture, Information Technology and Communication, and Mining, will establish programs for implementing environmental taxes, including on the use of water.

Source: Prepared by the author

For the government's part, the previously mentioned Sustainability Pact is directly related to the SDGs, which led us to setting certain goals, outlined in table 2:

TABLE 2. THE COLOMBIAN STATE'S
GOALS REGARDING CLIMATE CHANGE

PRESENT	FUTURE
• According to the National Inventory of Greenhouse Gases, direct total GHG emissions in 2014 were 236.97 million tons of CO_2-eq, of which approximately half (55%) originated from the AFOLU* sector, within which the main sources of emissions (36.4%) are deforestation and land degradation. Elsewhere, the energy sector is responsible for around 35% of emissions, of which the two main sources are the burning of fossil fuels in transportation and the emissions from energy industries.	• Reduce GHG emissions by 51% by 2030.
• In the last six years, an area of forest equivalent to 926,000 soccer fields has been lost. Currently, 701,000 hectares have been recovered with sustainable production and conservation systems (DNP et al., 2017).	• The goal is to double this number of hectares to 1.4 million, for restoration and sustainable agricultural, forestry and forest management systems. Furthermore, the aim is to halt deforestation with the planting of 180 million trees by 2022 (DNP et al., 2017).
• In Colombia, we consume 2.8 times more raw materials per unit of GDP than the average across countries in the Organization for Economic Co-operation and Development (OECD). Additionally, we have low water productivity (18.9 USD/m^3) and arable land productivity (33,200 USD/km^2), with limited technical assistance (reaching just 3% of the total of producers) (DNP et al., 2017). Furthermore, losses averaging 50% are registered in irrigation districts (DANE & IDEAM, 2015; CIAT, 2018).	• Decree 690 of 2021 regulates the sustainable management of non-timber-yielding forest products and wild flora. Similarly, the actions of programs such as *Visión Amazonía* and *Núcleas de Desarrollo Forestal* promote a forest development model based on the conservation of forests and the sustainable use of natural resources. The National Development Plan established a goal of a 30% reduction in the deforestation projected by IDEAM by 2022. The accumulated results since 2018 show an accumulated reduction of 28% on a national scale. The preliminary results of 2021 indicate a reduction of 30%, particularly in the departments of Meta, Caquetá and Guaviare. The goal for 2030 is to reach net deforestation of zero**.

PRESENT	FUTURE
• The illegal extraction of gold has affected 1,150 rivers and streams across the country (DNP et al., 2017). Mercury has contaminated the following rivers: Atrato (Chocó), Vichada (Meta), Acandí (Chocó), Caquetá (Caquetá), Yarí (Amazonas), Arroyohondo (Valle del Cauca), Simití (Santander), Barbacoas (Nariño) and Puerto Berrío (Magdalena).	• As part of its commitment to the Minamata Convention on Mercury, Colombia is working to become a country free from this heavy metal by 2023. Similarly, sustainable solutions will be built alongside the communities to reduce the social and environmental impacts of artisanal, small-scale gold extraction.
• 88% of natural disasters in the country are related to floods, landslides, droughts and mudslides.	• The technical-scientific entities must build and implement strategies to establish municipal territorial planning across the national territory. This way, the territories can be more resilient to natural phenomena and the impact of climate change.

*Agriculture, Forestry and Other Land Uses

**https://www.minambiente.gov.co/
noticias-minambiente/5206-acciones-ambientales-para-la-paz-una-prioridad-de-gobier-no-nacional

Source: Prepared by the author

Now, let's look at some of the goals from my government's four-year term, by indicator (figure 1):

FIGURE 1. FOUR-YEAR GOALS BY INDICATOR

1. Sustainability and the mitigation of climate change

Sector	Indicator	Base line	Four-year goal	Associated SDG (primary)	Associated SDG (secondary)
Agriculture and rural development	Areas with sustainable bovine rearing production systems	72,000 ha	147,000 ha	Responsible consumption and production	Climate action · Life on land
Transportation	Electric vehicles registered in the RUNT	1,695 (2016)	6,600	Affordable and clean energy	Climate action
Mines and energy	Energy intensity	3.70 (terajoules/ billion pesos 2005)	3.43 (terajoules/ billion pesos 2005)	Affordable and clean energy	Climate action
Environment and sustainable development	Rate of recycling and new use of waste	8.7%	12%	Responsible consumption and production	Climate action
Environment and sustainable development	Hazardous and special waste subject to post-consumption management	218,427 tons	565,995 tons	Responsible consumption and production	Good health and well-being · Climate action
Environment and sustainable development	Accumulated waste from GHG emissions, with respect to the national reference setting* (T)	0 tCO2eq	36 million tCO2eq	Climate action	Industry, innovation and infrastructure · Sustainable cities and communities
Environment and sustainable development	Monitored areas with a poor Water Quality Index (WQI)**	29	20	Clean water and sanitation	Life on land
Environment and sustainable development	Percentage of air quality monitoring stations which register annual concentrations below 30 µg/m3 of PM10 particulate matter***	22%	35%	Climate action	Industry, innovation and infrastructure · Sustainable cities and communities

* The goal may be adjusted in the event of modifications to the base year of the nationally-determined contribution.

** The monitored areas will be prioritized depending on the scale of the problem.

*** The air quality monitoring stations will be prioritized according to necessity.

T: Transformational Indicator / Sector Priority.

46

2. Biodiversity and natural riches

Sector	Indicator	Base line	Four-year goal	Associated SDG (primary)	Associated SDG (secondary)		
Environment and sustainable development	Areas under Payment for Environmental Services (PES) and incentive schemes	65,000 ha	260,000 ha	Life on land	Decent work and economic growth		
Environment and sustainable development	Percentage of unrepresented or under-represented ecosystems or ecosystemic analysis areas included in the SINAP over the four-year term	0%	15%	Life on land	Life below water		
Science, technology and innovation	New bioproducts registered by the Colombia Bio Program	84	126	Decent work and economic growth	Responsible consumption and production	Life on land	
Science, technology and innovation	New national scientific expeditions carried out with the support of Colciencias and partners	20	25	Industry, innovation and infrastructure	Decent work and economic growth	Responsible consumption and production	
Environment and sustainable development	Verified green businesses	429	1,865	Responsible consumption and production	Decent work and economic growth	Life on land	
Agriculture and rural development	Percentage of participation of the forest economy in the GDP	0.69%	1%	Life on land	Decent work and economic growth	Responsible consumption and production	
Environment and sustainable development	Areas under sustainable conservation systems (restoration*, forestry systems, sustainable forest management)	701,000 ha	1,402,900 ha	Life on land			
Environment and sustainable development	Percentage improvement in the management effectivity rate of protected areas	0%	20%	Life on land			

Continues on the next page

Sector	Indicator	Base line	Four-year goal	Associated SDG (primary)	Associated SDG (secondary)
Environment and sustainable development	Reducing the deforestation growth trend projected by IDEAM	0%	30%	Life on land	Zero hunger / Decent work and economic growth / Industry, innovation and infrastructure

* The goal includes 301,900 hectares in the restoration process.

Sector	Program	Indicator	Base line	Four-year goal	Associated SDG (primary)	Associated SDG (secondary)
Environment and sustainable development	Strengthening the environmental performance of production sectors	Number of zero deforestation agreements for the production chains of the agricultural sector that are in process (T)	2	5	Life on land	Zero hunger / Decent work and economic growth / Industry, innovation and infrastructure
Environment and sustainable development	Conservation of biodiversity and its ecosystem services	Collaborative platforms made up of the joining of public and private investments and actions around drainage basins	0	8	Life on land	Peace, justice and strong institutions

T: Transformational Indicator / Sector Priority.

48

3. Knowledge and prevention for disaster risk management and adaptation to climate change

Sector	Indicator	Base line	Four-year goal	Associated SDG (primary)	Associated SDG (secondary)
President's office	Number of people affected by recurring events (per 100,000 inhabitants)	1,048	987	No poverty	Sustainable cities and communities Climate action
Environment and sustainable development	Environmental authorities adopting the Damage Assessment and Analysis of Environmental Needs methodology	0	8	Climate action	
Environment and sustainable development	Percentage of departments implementing climate adaptation initiatives guided by the environmental authorities	0%	100%	Climate action	No poverty Sustainable cities and communities
Agriculture and Rural Development	Area with prioritized agricultural production systems which implement initiatives for adaptation to climate change	260,626 ha	398,175 ha	Zero hunger	Climate action
Environment and Sustainable Development. Program: Information and environmental knowledge management	Percentage of the National Climate Change System implemented	0%	100%	Climate action	Partnerships for the goals

Note: Six production systems will be prioritized: rice, corn, banana, sugar cane, potatoes, and bovine livestock.

49

4. Modern environmental institutions, social ownership of biodiversity and management of socio-environmental conflicts

Sector	Indicator	Base line	Four-year goal	Associated SDG (primary)	Associated SDG (secondary)
Environment and sustainable development	Rate of evaluation of institutional performance of the Regional Autonomous Corporations	84%	90%	Peace, justice and strong institutions	
Environment and sustainable development	Implemented inter-ministerial and production agreements and agendas	0	8		
Environment and sustainable development	Percentage of environmental license requests for which the ANLA is responsible which are responded to within the timeframe established in current guidelines	75 %	95%	Life on land	Affordable and clean energy Decent work and economic growth Industry, innovation and infrastructure

SOURCE: National Planning Department (2019).

EVERYBODY'S RESPONSIBILITY

Colombia is one of the most diverse countries on the planet. Fifty-two percent of its territory is covered by forests: the Amazon, Pacific and Andean regions alone are home to 94% of these forests. Furthermore, the national territory contains almost 3 million hectares of paramos (high Andean moorlands), with 22 million hectares of wetlands. Its coastline stretches 3,330 km and its waters, home to highly biodiverse ecosystems, cover 892,102 km^2 (Invemar, 2018).

These figures show the immense biodiversity of the nation, but also the great vulnerability of this natural capital, which is not infinite. In fact, deforestation and the degradation of ecosystems, as well as GHG emissions, have seen a rise in recent years. It is vital to conserve our biodiversity, because it bears the weight of the population's living means as well as a significant part of the country's production system (figure 2).

FIGURE 2. MAP OF DEFORESTATION 2015-2017

Departmental border

Deforestation 2015-2017

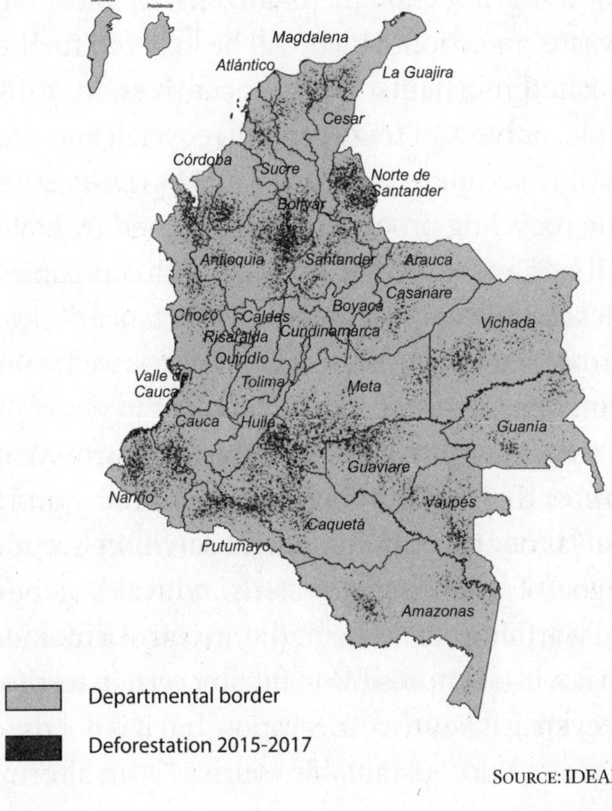

SOURCE: IDEAM (2018)

The "Produce while preserving, preserve while producing" strategy does not just depend on the sustainable use of resources and the transformation or creation of inclusive and innovative businesses, but also on each one of our inhabitants. Together we must care for and preserve the ecosystems. That is why we insist on the importance of the Sustainability Pact, which promotes investigation and innovation in the development of sustainable packaging and in giving a use to materials which are hard to exploit.

But this is not enough. As citizens, we must recycle this waste, an action which will be fostered further by established mechanisms and incentives. In 2018, for example, only 5% of textiles were recycled and reused, when the maximum potential was 53% (DNP, 2018).

The recycling process is strengthened by environmental culture campaigns, in which both companies and families can become aware of the importance of cleaning and protecting our natural surroundings, as well as understanding the impact of actions such as the yearly planting of trees and the social valuation of nature. We must remember that it is everybody's responsibility, and that, as small as our contribution might seem, we are adding to the goal of producing zero GHGs and avoiding the continued warming of Earth and the arrival of a moment in which it will be impossible to inhabit certain territories.

Recycling is key to conservation, but it is not the only thing we can do. Sustainable tourism is an alternative which allows for a better use of natural capital and which represents great development potential: for example, between 2015 and 2017, visits to protected areas increased by 70%. At the same time, this has brought with it the challenge of creating and strengthening training programs, connectivity products and services, sustainable infrastructure and a carrying capacity which is truly sustainable.

Now, we can recycle, we can modify some of our habits and we can also promote new activities which contribute to the common goal of saving the planet. However, it is understandable that there will be some reservations when proposing such radical changes, and we cannot plan or carry anything out without having the conviction that it will not affect our quality of life, the local community's income or the national economy. So, if we are considering modifying the way we use natural resources when we travel, for example, we must have a very clear strategy so that the tourism sector does not suffer. How, then, do we promote sustainable tourism as the engine for regional development? The pact considers various strategies for consolidating a responsible tourism model through education, awareness and culture-building programs.

Ecotourism implies a balance between nature and adventure and, in order to develop it, strategies have been put in place to attract investment and promote businesses with quality and sustainability certificates among tourist destinations and operators. All of those linked to the sector should not only strengthen their technical abilities, they should also train in sustainable development and patrimony. That way, they can encourage visitors to be more conscious of the importance of protecting cultural and natural attractions.

Investigation does not simply promote a better use of materials and travel experiences in protected areas. It also allows citizens to gain access to open databases and reports in order to understand more about the bioeconomy and bioprospecting, the characteristics of bioproducts, the new species registers, community forestry programs, inter-region and local initiatives, and the implementation of technology in the agricultural sector, among other things. In general, the results of investigations allow for a better understanding of climate change, in order to be able to make better decisions regarding the adaptation of all sectors, and provide education which is sensitive to the environmental emergency.

Part of this better understanding of biodiversity can be seen in the decisions we have taken in confronting the deterioration of marine ecosystems. Colombia is an oceanic biodiversity powerhouse, which is why our Ocean Regions Pact seeks to: conserve and restore marine ecosystems; promote scientific and technological innovation and the application of innovation to the understanding and development of the oceans; make the fishing industry more competitive and responsible; and increase the cargo potential and logistics capacity of the country's ports.

Our oceans have a unique development potential. They are one of our most important engines for growth and equality. That is why we must put all our resolve into caring for them, preserving them and using their resources in a sustainable and responsible way. How can we do that? In the same way as with all environmental resources: conserving and taking care of the diversity which, in this case, the marine, coastal and island ecosystems provide us with.

For example, according to Invemar (2018), "unsuitable use and contamination have decimated their biodiversity and fish resources, with a notable effect on coral reefs". Coral reef and algae habitats have deteriorated, and not only due to the effect of climate change and the acidification of the oceans. The loss of sharks has also led to their decline, as have the losses caused by commercial fisheries. That is why, in November 2020, the government prohibited the traditional and industrial fishing of sharks in Colombia's waters. This animal is far more important than the majority of the population realizes: it is at the top of the food chain but, more importantly, it contributes to a marine balance, as it keeps the smallest species at their trophic level and regulates the ocean's health indicators. By eliminating its presence from the coral reef ecosystems, other predators, such as groupers, will multiply and feed on herbivores. And with fewer herbivores, the seaweed will spread and the coral will be unable to compete with it, so the ecosystem will become dominated by algae and the reef's survival will be threatened. This is why the artisanal fishing communities were given access to payments for environmental services which guarantees them a source of income.

Furthermore, as a government, we decided to entirely prohibit the fishing of sting rays and sharks and the practice of shark finning (removing the fins of live sharks in order to sell them), as we understand that sharks help to guarantee the diversity and habitats of species by eating sick species and maintaining the balance of the ecosystem.

Apart from protecting sharks, it is vital for Colombia to be able to recover, rehabilitate and restore the live coral cover. Corals protect us from hurricane seasons and if we do not do anything to save the coral reserves, they could disappear by 2050. They are also strategic ecosystems upon which the economies of local communities depend, as they provide food security. In the words of Phanor Montoya, director of *Corales de Paz* (Corals of Peace): "Coral reefs are a strategic ecosystem for the planet, not only because they are home to one in every four species found in the oceans, but because they also provide 370 billion dollars a year to the global economy. This sum comes mainly from recreation, coastal protection services and food production. Coral reefs are structures which change the conditions of the sea, of the depths of the oceans".

Aware of this situation, the government decided to invest USD $2,224,000[3] in the "Restoring a million corals for Colombia" program between 2021 and 2022. With the collaboration of various ministries and international cooperation, the program seeks to recover 200 hectares of the country's coral reef, and will focus its efforts on intervening in and conserving the following areas of coral (figure 3):

- The integrated management district of the Seaflower protected marine area and the McBean Lagoon National Park in the San Andrés, Providencia and Santa Catalina archipelago.

- The Tayrona National Park and Taganga Bay (Magdalena).

- The Rosario and San Bernardo Corals National Park, Barú Island, Palma Island and Fuerte Island (Bolívar).

- Rincón del Mar (Sucre).

- Acandí Wildlife Sanctuary, Playón and Playona (Chocó's Caribbean).

- On the Pacific coast, the Utría National Park (Chocó), and the Gorgona National Park (Cauca).

---

3   Throughout this book, amounts have been converted from Colombian Pesos (COP), using the Representative Market Rate of the day, which, at the time of translation, was 3,800 COP to 1 USD. Values presented hereafter are in United States Dollars.

FIGURE 3. MAP OF CORAL AREAS

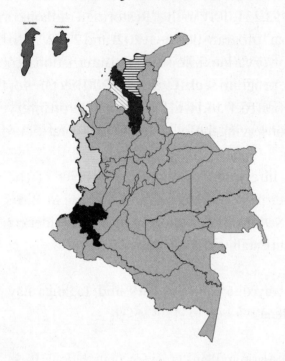

The integrated management district of the Seaflower protected marine area and the McBean Lagoon National Park in the San Andrés, Providencia and Santa Catalina archipelago.

The Rosario and San Bernardo Corals National Park, Barú Island, Palma Island and Fuerte Island (Bolívar).

The Tayrona National Park and Taganga Bay (Magdalena).

Rincón del Mar (Sucre).

Acandí Wildlife Sanctuary, Playón and Playona (Chocó's Caribbean).

On the Pacific coast, the Utría National Park (Chocó), and the Gorgona National Park (Cauca).

SOURCE: Ministry of Environment and Sustainable Development (2021).

The recovery of corals will take place through coral gardening, which involves nurseries attached to steel structures, or microfragmenting. The first technique takes naturally-fragmented coral as a seed and grows it underwater. The second technique grows thousands of coral fragments in farms or laboratories, which can then be directly transplanted onto the coral reef. We can create 100,000 fragments of species in 40 ocean-based nurseries, and 900,000 fragments, including massive coral species, through microfragmenting.

Furthermore, with regards to the riches of our seas, we have set the following challenges:

- Strengthening existing institutions in order to boost the development of the oceans.

- Mitigating coastal erosion, which generates impacts on the population, infrastructure and coastal and marine ecosystems.

- Strengthening the country's fishing potential.

- Increasing the levels of comprehensive maritime security.

- Increasing the logistical capacity of ports.

No action is without consequence. The solution can begin at any moment: rethinking tourism, caring for the oceans, consuming in a more conscious fashion, recycling, giving clothes a second use, car sharing, etc. Furthermore, when we come together as people, when we all contribute, nothing can stop us. That is why reaching the goal of zero emissions should be one of the reasons to stick together as a country.

Rural actions: how to change the world from the countryside

Colombia is, without doubt, a megadiverse country. In 2022, 52% of its surface area is covered by forests, but human activity, coupled with complex territorial dynamics, have accelerated the loss of nearly 3 million hectares of natural forest between 2001 and 2020.

Controlling deforestation and sustainably managing forests implies a cross-cutting commitment and the participation of all regions, particularly in rural areas where there are pending tasks in terms of: 1) converting agricultural, livestock and fishing production processes; 2) implementing better management of drinking and sewage water, and 3) promoting territorial planning based on ensuring territories are more resilient to floods, landslides, drought and avalanches, among other urgent strategies for mitigating the impact of climate change.

The formulation of policies and the implementation of the National Development Plan are not enough if the communities living in the countryside, and who are already suffering from the consequences of the degradation of the ecosystems, do not participate. Achievements in ecosystem management in Colombia are an example of this: around 35,000 hectares are already part of sustainable forest management systems, thanks to the joint work of local communities and strategic allies, and fourteen departmental forest roundtables have been set up for the local management of forests.

With the National Economic and Social Policy (CONPES, for its Spanish acronym) document, "National policy for the control of deforestation and sustainable management of forests", approved in January 2021, we outlined a ten-year path for promoting the sustainable use of natural resources, the forest economy and community development in 150 municipalities located in the territories suffering the greatest loss of vegetation cover.

Sustainable production implies stabilizing the limits of the agricultural frontiers with actions aimed at stopping the occupation and possession of land in biodiverse areas, exercising territorial control in order to reduce illegal dynamics which have an impact on deforestation and implementing the management and tracking of forest resources. Above all, we must support social investment, so that communities can exercise sustainable forest governance in order to protect and conserve natural resources.

The exact actions aimed at combating deforestation and mitigating the impact of the climate on the Amazon in 2021 are the following:

- The Jungle School: environmental education for 600 rural families in the Amazon.

- Payments for environmental services programs, green credits, production and rural extension projects: recruitment of 4,102 rural families with an investment of $9.21 million.

- Projects by indigenous communities: $5.32 million will be available to 17,263 families in order to develop initiatives which protect and conserve the environment, based on their world view and ancestral knowledge.

- The formulation of 1,573 conservation contracts and formalization of property.

- Structuring the Inter-Modal Transport Plan in the Amazon.

- The formulation of Caquetá's Electrification Plan.

- Two tourism projects for the La Macarena Special Management Area.

- The strategic Administrative Planning Region (RAP, for its Spanish acronym) of the Amazon, with an investment of $2.74 million.

- Forest ordinance: forest usage, control and vigilance, and environmental education covering 70,000 hectares, with an investment of $1.84 million.

- Recovery of 21,000 hectares affected by deforestation in the national parks of the Amazon biome.

- Improving trails and systems for attention to and observation of species in the National Parks system, with the aim of promoting ecotourism, particularly in 36 parks.

- Strengthening the tools for fighting against ecocide and criminal practices which threaten the environment; these tools include CONPES, the *Visión Amazonía* program and *Campaña Artemisa*.

- Strengthening the coal market, green businesses and the circular economy in the country, with the aim of making progress with the "Produce while preserving, and preserve while producing" strategy.

- Silvopastoral sowing in 100,000 hectares over 18 months, with the aim of contributing to reforestation and the generation of sustainable practices in activities such as livestock rearing.

LAKES AND ENVIRONMENTAL FRONTIERS FOR LIFE

As an example of the strategy we are putting into place, let us look at the case of the Tarapoto Lakes, in Puerto Nariño, Amazonas, where the processes of reforestation are already showing the first results. The hands of 289 families planted around 12,000 native trees, which will protect this collection of lakes, allowing for the production of more fruits for the fish and also for human consumption.

Furthermore, the families of the communities of Atacarí, Siete de Agosto, Boyahuassu and Naranjales have committed to controlling and monitoring the state of the planted trees, with the aim of ensuring that the reforestation is effective. This community work will be supported by forest engineers who will be permanently monitoring through geopositioning.

In addition, with the support of the National Environmental System (SINA, for its Spanish acronym), CorpoAmazonía and the Omacha Foundation, the communities have been able to plant acai, moriche palm fruits, embira fruits, genipapo fruits, tirameo fruits and bacuri fruits in order to counteract deforestation. The recovery of the Tarapoto Lakes is a priority, given that it is the only complex of wetlands in the Colombian Amazon which has been declared a Ramsar site, that is to say that it has

64

the international recognition of the Ramsar Convention for the conservation of wetlands and sustainable use of resources. Furthermore, the Tarapoto Lakes are a birthplace of pink dolphins.

Caring for biodiversity implies the development of sustainable projects, and planting trees is just one of the diverse strategies which have allowed communities to understand ecosystems and their ecological structure. Another of the challenges is learning how to use the natural resources provided by the Amazon in a sustainable fashion. Some good news in this regard are the projects developed as part of the framework of the "Leticia BiodiverCity" strategy for managing natural, cultural and ethnic riches in line with the needs of the communities and the territory. For example, with the support of the Sinchi Institute, the teaching of sustainable consumption habits has been promoted, as have the local production of biodegradable packaging using Amazonian resources, the development of pisciculture with native species and the characterization of urban wetlands, among other actions which benefit the locals.

Another good example is the Abrigue Project, which, as outline in figure 4, benefits populations in areas on the forest frontier in Meta, Chocó and Caquetá.

It is also important to mention that in 2020, thanks to the National Environmental Zoning Plan, 139,100 hectares were protected in Caquetá, a department made up of 72.4% of areas of environmental importance and 50%

of whose territory is covered by ecosystem services. All of these areas are at risk, due to deforestation and agricultural extension. That is why it has been vital to implement mechanisms for updating the use and extension of special environmental areas, to delimit the agricultural frontier, formalize land titles and, especially, to generate activities which strike a balance between human activity and the environment.

FIGURE 4. ABRIGUE PROJECT

For example, we set up the Abrigue Project, which aims to benefit

4,000 rural families
and indigenous and Afro-Colombian communities living in areas on the forest frontier.

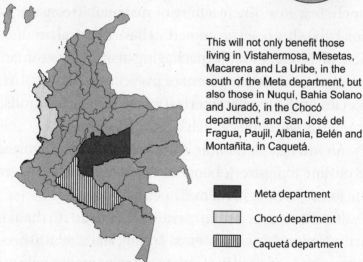

This will not only benefit those living in Vistahermosa, Mesetas, Macarena and La Uribe, in the south of the Meta department, but also those in Nuquí, Bahia Solano and Juradó, in the Chocó department, and San José del Fragua, Paujil, Albania, Belén and Montañita, in Caquetá.

▨ Meta department

▨ Chocó department

▨ Caquetá department

SOURCE: Ministry of Environment and Sustainable Development (2021).

66

ECOLOGICALLY-EFFICIENT STOVES AND RESIDUAL BIOMASS IN ORDER TO REDUCE EMISSIONS

The substitution of traditional stoves for ecologically-efficient stoves is one of Colombia's commitments on the road to reducing GHG emissions by 51% before 2030. The installation of a million ecologically-efficient stoves over the next decade will represent a reduction of approximately 2.29 million tons of CO_2 in the year 2030, which is currently emitted as a result of combustion inefficiencies and high levels of firewood consumption.

The "Installation of ecologically-efficient stoves in rural dwellings project" methodology aims to standardize the design and implementation of efficient wood-burning cooking technologies, which minimize the impact on natural surroundings and people's health by reducing emissions which contaminate the air, and contributing to better air quality and a reduction in GHG emissions. Thus, they contribute to the mitigation of and adaptation to climate change, and promote the efficient, sustainable and rational use of firewood.

In Cundinamarca, 1,500 families living in seven municipalities in the jurisdiction of the Autonomous Regional Corporation of Guavio (Corpoguavio) are already enjoying the benefits of these new ecologically-efficient stoves which, as well as minimizing the impact on climate change, and thanks to greater energy efficiency, reduce the quantity of firewood needed and guarantee quality of life and health, as they are fitted with gas extractors.

Now, this project becomes even more powerful if it is added to other ecologically-efficient strategies, such as circular allotments. These are not just about reducing GHGs, but also rescuing ancestral agricultural traditions which allow for a better management of natural resources and healthier diets. Collaborative work in these municipalities has promoted alternatives for family agriculture, such as sustainable production in small areas, a reduction of 80% in water consumption, recycling of nutrients and the preservation of the conditions and structures of soil.

Considering that everything has a chain reaction, the installation of ecologically-efficient stoves does not just help us reduce the amount of CO_2 getting into the atmosphere; this strategy has also been key to protecting the country's paramos. For example, in the Las Tinajas paramo, in Valle del Cauca, this project has been carried out by members of the Triunfo Cristal Páez indigenous community, the Afro-Colombian community and the Ebenezer Farmers' Association, with the support of the Autonomous Regional Corporation of Valle del Cauca and the Ministry of Environment. There, residual water treatment systems (SITAR, for their Spanish acronym) and solar panels have been implemented in order to further protect the complex of nine lagoons and 18,400 hectares which make up this vital territory.

In Valle del Cauca, more than $395,000 has been allocated to implementing 120 ecologically-efficient stoves, strengthening 21 sustainable production systems, building three community allotments with a vegetable production and implementation plan, and carrying out 33 workshops on the suitable management of natural resources. With this, we are not only looking to protect our paramos, but also biodiversity and ecosystem services in the catchment areas of the National Protective Forest Reserves (RFPN, for their Spanish acronym), particularly the Dagua, Amaime and Tuluá catchment areas.

As well as the ecologically-efficient stoves, it is vital to manage another large source of GHG emissions generated by the agricultural and livestock sectors: residual biomass. Organic waste can be made use of thanks to the circular economy, thus reducing its environmental, social and economic impact. In the agricultural sector, for example, there is post-harvest waste, such as the sugar cane plants which, after being processed, can be turned into *panela* (raw sugar cane); there is also biomass waste from the livestock sector, such as manure from pigs and chickens, which can be transformed into new products, such as fertilizers and materials for degraded soil. This exploitation opportunity can generate green businesses, a circular economy, a reduction in CO_2 emissions, and responsible consumption and production.

Each year in Colombia, many tons of organic waste are generated. Sugar cane, for example, generates 19 million tons; plantain, 16.5 million; raw sugar cane, 8.4 million; and the poultry and pork subsectors, 8.7 million tons. All of this organic waste can be used to revive degraded soil and efficiently make use of resources in the production cycles of the agricultural, commercial, consumption, and specialized waste management sectors. Thus we can reduce GHG emissions generated by the uncontrolled decomposition of organic matter.

Urban actions: how to change the world from the city

Colombia is a country which seeks to prepare its cities for the current and future socio-environmental challenges, for facing climate change and the challenges set by developing as a low-carbon and climate-resistant country, all at the same time as showing concern for improving the well-being and quality of life of its people in environmental, social and economic terms.

Biodiverciudades (biodiverse cities), the national government's initiative and part of the National Development Plan, with the tag-line "Produce while preserving, and preserve while producing", is a strategy which seeks to contribute to the transformation of cities whose development is focused on achieving urban, environmental sustainability, in dialogue and harmony with nature.

In general terms, it could be said that a biodiverse city is a city which recognizes, prioritizes and integrates biodiversity and its benefits into sustainable urban-regional development. The strategy aims to make cities capable of caring for their natural surroundings, in order to improve the quality of life of their inhabitants – guaranteeing well-being, equality and social inclusion – and promoting low-carbon development, in order to contribute to adaptation and resilience to the climate, as part of climate change management.

This strategy focuses on three prongs:

- *Sustainable development.* It seeks to promote economic opportunities, social well-being and the protection of the environment, with the aim of transforming cities in an integrated fashion, guaranteeing the same opportunities in the future.

- *Urban-regional.* The development of cities must take into account a wider perspective of the territory, such that any identified needs take into account regional conditions.

- *Prospective.* It aims to prepare cities for the future. It hopes to immediately contribute to the comprehensive and gradual transformation of cities, taking into account the principal urban challenges and environmental needs.

Currently, the Ministry of Environment and Sustainable Development has decided to start the *Biodiverciudades* initiative in 14 cities across the country: Barranquilla, Leticia, Medellín, Bucaramanga, Quibdó, San Andrés and Providencia Islands, Barrancabermeja, Manizales, Montería, Armenia, Yopal, Pereira and Pasto.

Not only is it a moral and ecological imperative to place biodiversity at the center of city planning and development, it is also necessary in order to highlight the importance of biodiversity to renewing the urban economy.

In the cities of the Amazon, for example, projects which include biodiversity in development have been pursued. In Leticia, clean transportation, and the reduction, reuse and recycling of waste through a circular economy have been promoted. Other Colombian cities have also joined this program of transformation into green, resilient urban centers in order to meet the Sustainable Development Goals and mitigate climate change. Barranquilla, San Andrés and Providencia Islands, Montería, Medellín, Quibdó, Bucaramanga, Villavicencio, Manizales, Barrancabermeja, Armenia, Pasto and Yopal are opting for sustainable consumption, the development of a sustainable economy and territorial planning.

Now, the commitment of cities implies an investment in sustainable infrastructure, environmental education, air quality, a circular economy and BioTrade. Therefore, the Ministry of Environment has prioritized the consolidation of the National Air Quality Monitoring Network, guaranteeing a new air quality monitoring stations system for biodiverse cities. This is linked to a national urban biodiversity monitoring program, based on citizen participation scientific activities, the consolidation of a program of 1,000 garden centers which will be built in Colombian schools, guaranteeing the students' contribution to the ecological recovery of cities, and the structuring of 86 projects for public spaces, ecotourism, sustainable constructions and waste management.

Let's remember that, if we understand territorial needs in our climate actions and take ownership of the knowledge of the biodiversity that surrounds us, we can contribute to a sustainable recovery. So, what follows is an explanation of how the cities are contributing to green, resilient reactivation:

- Consolidating an economic reactivation CONPES.

- Updating the Nationally Determined Contribution on meeting the goal of a 51% reduction in GHG emissions by 2030: it includes 196 concrete actions, objectives, policies and measures for mitigation, adaptation and implementation means (finances, planning, and development and transfer of technologies).

- Building information capacities, education and systems.

- Generating 400,000 jobs in programs for planting 180 million trees, bioeconomy programs, 4.0

industry development, and zero deforestation and innovation strategies.

Additionally, in order to transform cities, their infrastructure must be more resilient to climate change. Therefore, the Ministry of Environment and Sustainable Development and the National Infrastructure Agency (ANI, for its Spanish acronym) defined the conditions for works in a call for summons, which include: 1) technical, financial and economic aspects of the transport infrastructure contracts; 2) actions for risk mitigation, adaptation and management for construction endorsed by the ANI, and 3) climate change and risk management measures in public works. Using the most vulnerable projects across the national territory as a starting point, the country will have a guide for planning infrastructure with sustainable processes which incorporate new technologies and innovation, and whose construction and operation will contribute to a reduction in GHG emissions.

As well as pursuing sustainable infrastructure works, Colombian cities have a tool for measuring and managing emissions generated by activities in urban areas and surrounding areas. With the "Inventory Guide for Greenhouse Gas Emissions", territories can identify, calculate and report emissions, and thus formulate policies for their reduction. Currently, Medellín and Cali are updating their emissions inventory; as for Montería and Pereira, they already have the most up-to-date urban GHG inventory, and in the future these results will help mitigate the effects of climate change and contribute to lowering the temperature. The plan is to make use of the guide in all of the country's cities.

In addition to the guide, we have also planned 48 future actions in urban areas, which will help to reduce 3.5 million tons of CO_2 by 2030. With the support of the World Resources Institute (WRI), the World Wide Fund for Nature (WWF), and the Ministry of Trade, Industry and Tourism, the Ministry of Environment and Sustainable Development developed a project for identifying what 16 cities can contribute to reducing GHG emissions. These 48 future climate change projects will improve processes and use in the following areas:

- 43% - Replacing fuels and technology for a more efficient use of energy in industrial processes.

- 21% - Installation of solar panels for a sustainable management of electricity and hydrocarbons.

- 30% - Electrification of the transport fleets in cities and companies.

- 6% - Replacing lighting in buildings.

The quantification of GHG emissions is vital for implementing strategies for their reduction, and in order to do that, we must follow the recently-published national guide of inventories for cities in Colombia. However, different studies have proven that simply using the car less or reducing the number of flights is not enough to reach the longed-for zero anytime soon. In the first months of the pandemic, for example, CO_2 emissions dropped considerably, but not enough for alarm bells to stop ringing. During that period of cars and planes sitting idle, or less gas and fossil fuels being burned, we only dropped our gas emissions by 5%. That means that we went from 51 billion tons to 49 billion, and although that is not enough, it is undoubtedly progress that we should be able to maintain.

The path towards environmental security and preservation

The conservation of Colombia's biodiversity is vital. Positioning natural riches as a strategic asset implies meeting clear objectives for protecting them from deforestation and processes of degradation. Not only do ecosystems need to be conserved, it is also necessary to implement comprehensive actions in environmentally-strategic areas, including the communities that inhabit them, generating incentives and payments for environmental services and driving the development of sustainability-based products and services.

With the aim of ensuring that the strategy for conserving biodiversity is seen through, the National Development Plan 2018-2022 includes an intervention for exercising territorial control, in which the Ministry of Defense and the Ministry of Environment and Sustainable Development have joined forces in order to prevent and deal with illegal dynamics which directly affect ecosystems. These activities are related, among other things, to the illegal exploitation of mineral deposits, marine contamination and illegal fishing, the illicit use of natural resources, the illegal wildlife trade, genetic and hydro-biological resources, and mistreatment of animals, which occur in priority conservation areas.

CAMPAÑA ARTEMISA

This military strategy to stop deforestation was launched during a trip to the municipality of La Macarena, Meta, in April 2019. This area is important for preservation because it was under the control of the FARC, whose activities relating to drug trafficking had an impact on the deforestation of the ecosystems. The campaign is designed to fulfill different objectives: first, to stop the "deforesting hemorrhage" that we have witnessed over the last few years; secondly, to recover our tropical rainforest and other forest ecosystems; and thirdly, to bring those who are behind that deforestation culture to justice.

As part of this campaign, security forces have carried out 12 operations, centered around the national parks of the Amazon and Orinoco, including Chiribiquete, La Paya, Tinigua, the Los Picachos mountain range, the La Macarena range and the Amazon Forest Reserve Area, declared a reserve in Law 2 of 1959. Thanks to the execution of ten operations as part of the Artemisa Campaign, by March 2021, 14,538 hectares of previously-deforested land had been recovered; by September 2021, this figure had surpassed 15,200 hectares (see figure 5).

FIGURE 5. *ARTEMISA'S OPERATIONS*

Artemisa's operations have focused on the national parks of the Amazon and Orinoco, including Chiribiquete, La Paya, Tinigua, Picachos, La Macarena and the Amazon Forest Reserve Zone.

Amazon

Orinoco

Serranía de La Macarena

Picachos

Tinigua

Serranía de Chiribiquete

La Paya

SOURCE: Ministry of Defense (2021).

In conjunction with the National District Attorney's Office, Artemisa has led to:

- The capture of 96 people by court order or being caught in the act for various environmental crimes.

- The disqualification of 37 constructions, 5 illegal roads and 2 bridges in areas of natural protection.

- The seizure of 32 chainsaws, 7 scythes, 7 vehicles and 13 cattle branding irons.

STRATEGIES FOR DEFENDING AND PROTECTING NATURAL RESOURCES

Our country's defense sector has a hefty commitment to protecting the environment, based on its constitutional mandate to guarantee security. Given that our greatest treasure is our biodiversity, its policy of legality, undertaking and equality seeks to defend and preserve water and biodiversity as strategic assets of the nation. Similarly, through Resolution 4455 of 2018, the Defense Sector's Environmental Policy was adopted, which establishes the efforts of internal environmental management to ensure that defense actions are thorough and in line with the national environmental policy for supporting environmental authorities in terms of security.

Working with the Armed Forces and National Police Force, the Ministry of Defense takes on the task of protecting natural resources, using a multidimensional security approach. Its fundamental mission is to support and guide environmental authorities in the defense of strategic assets, as well as preventing future damages resulting from environmental contamination, and the control of exploitation areas and corridors for the trafficking of natural resources.

So, the Ministry of Defense's work is carried out following three main strategic lines, as shown in table 3.

TABLE 3. STRATEGIC LINES FOR THE DEFENSE OF THE ENVIRONMENT

ACTION LINE	SPECIFIC OBJECTIVES
Supporting the National Environmental System and knowledge development	• The defense and care for renewable natural resources and the environment, under the framework of inter-institutional integration which seeks to protect biodiversity in natural forests, protected areas and strategic ecosystems. • Promoting the development of studies and investigations which contribute to the conservation and preservation of marine, river, land and air ecosystems.
Internal environmental management	• Promoting the conservation of biodiversity and the sustainable use of ecosystem services, through infrastructure projects for the design and planning of territorial usage. Armed Forces directives seek to ensure that planning areas and entities responsible for the development of infrastructure works generate and strengthen guidelines for sustainable construction. • Applying principles in the construction of green, sustainable infrastructure in agreements with government institutions. • Ensuring that infrastructure built from 2018 onwards meets the environmental parameters set by the relevant authorities, including projects carried out by military engineers.

ACTION LINE	SPECIFIC OBJECTIVES
Internal environmental management	• Ensuring the adoption of institutional practices which permit the separation and recycling of waste for its subsequent reuse and reduction. • Including sustainability criteria from previous studies. Requiring all contractors to hand in post-consumption plans, as well as meeting environmental regulations and demonstrating an adequate final arrangement of waste with certificates. • Implementing plans, projects or programs which improve processes of catchment, treatment, storage and distribution of water resources. • Acquiring efficient technologies and promoting the use of renewable energy sources, thus reducing GHG emissions and the excessive consumption of resources.
Carrying out military and police operations framed by the protection of human rights and the environment	• Supporting all actions which seek to eradicate illicit activities in the country's ecosystems. • Supporting environmental authorities in reducing the impact of a loss of natural forests resulting from various causes and agents of deforestation. • Dealing with illegal fishing activities in the seas and rivers.

SOURCE: Prepared by the author

At this point, I feel that it is important to share with you some graphs regarding crimes against the environment and natural resources (figure 6).

FIGURE 6. CRIMES AGAINST THE ENVIRONMENT

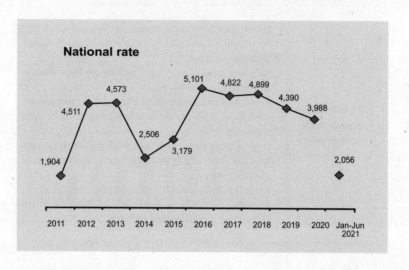

National rate

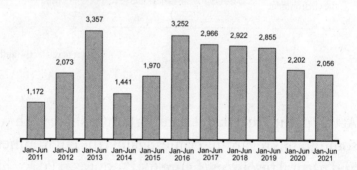

Comparison, year to date

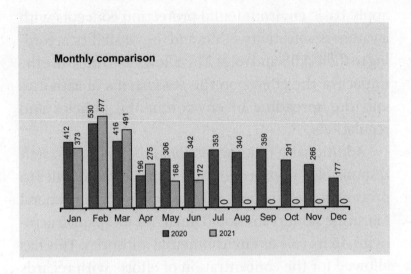

Monthly comparison

	Jan	Feb	Mar	Apr	May	Jun	Jul	Aug	Sep	Oct	Nov	Dec
2020	412	530	416	196	306	342	353	340	359	291	266	177
2021	373	577	491	275	168	172	0	0	0	0	0	0

Variation, year to date

Jan-Jun 2020	Jan-Jun 2021	Abs. Var.	Var. %
2,202	2,056	-146	-7 %

*Preliminary figures subject to change

SOURCE: National Police Force (2021).

Elsewhere, the National Cleaner Production Policy has allowed institutions to conduct their activities and operations using sustainable resource management and having the lowest impact possible on the environment. A cross-cutting environmental education line has also been established, allowing public sector workers to apply basic environmental protection concepts with awareness, sensitivity, ethics and responsibility, according to their skills and roles. This allows us to measure the impact of the effects on the ecosystems of activities and the spreading of environmental policies and regulations.

Additionally, training sessions are provided to staff responsible for inspection and supervision in order to prevent contamination, as is the case with the General Maritime Administration (Dimar, for its Spanish acronym), in its role as environmental authority. This has allowed for the concentration of efforts with regards training institutions which make up the Defense sector in topics related to prevention and environmental protection.

Furthermore, the Ministry of Defense's General Management Unit, through the Administrative Section, responsible for internal environmental management, designed and implemented the national Zero Paper strategy, to replace the use of paper with electronic means for sending, saving and following up on documentation. At the same time, this contributes to the implementation of the objectives of the national Sustainable Public Purchases program.

In order to promote the transition from fossil fuels and complements to alternative energy, a decision was made to implement energy generation systems with a minimal production of contaminating gases, especially in isolated areas which contain strategic ecosystems and which have high risks of environmental impact. This way, alternative energy contributes to helping a percentage of the most disadvantaged members of the population prosper, while we also care for the planet. Now, we know that the sources of renewable energy which currently exist (mainly solar and wind power) contribute to mitigating the problem of gas emissions. However, the production of electricity represents just 27% of all GHG emissions. That is why we cannot forget that, in order to avoid a climate disaster, we must:

• Reach zero emissions, as utopian as that sounds.

• Speed up the renewable energy tools we currently have at our disposal.

• Invest in technological development which will allow us to reduce the emission of gases.

Another relevant topic is the deforestation of the nation's strategic ecosystems, which has sped up, in part due to the rise in illegal activities associated with the extraction and exploitation of minerals, forest resources and illicit crops. According to González et al. (2016), "between 2005 and 2014, illicit crops were the cause of the deforestation of 17,562 hectares", mainly in the departments of Norte de Santander, Nariño, Cauca, Caquetá and Putumayo. Luckily, results in this field have been overwhelming, with the recognition of illicit crop eradication programs and support for crop substitution programs, increasing attention levels in the protected areas and territories that make up the National Parks System. For its part, the Artemisa Campaign has included a special chapter for combating illegal felling, as part of its actions to counteract the illegal trade of wild flora and fauna.

One of the focus areas of the Artemisa Campaign is protecting environmental patrimony. The defense and protection of environmental resources involves an inter-institutional effort to stop the rise in deforestation, recover the tropical rainforests and woods, and penalize the criminals responsible for deforestation.

Additionally, with the support of other state agencies, the defense sector is resolved to eliminating the effects on natural resources of the illicit extraction of minerals, an activity which involves criminal structures related to drug trafficking. The actions of the Armed Forces and police have been focused on counteracting the environmental impacts of terrorist activities, as well as safeguarding the human rights of the civilian population and ethnic groups.

PENALIZING ENVIRONMENTAL CRIMES

In order to conserve and protect nature, it is necessary to strengthen the national strategy for defending our natural resources with laws which penalize deforestation and actions which put our ecosystems at risk. In order to do this, the Ministry of Environment and Sustainable Development, Ministry of Justice, Interior Ministry and the National District Attorney's Office created a bill on environmental crimes. Thus, it is possible to take measures to counteract the promotion and financing of deforestation, the illegal wildlife trade and the financing of invasions into areas of special ecological importance, among other things. The law gives the District Attorney's Office the tools for prosecuting those responsible for degrading our ecosystems. The measures include removing the right to set up and open businesses.

Although the approval of this law is, in itself, a great achievement in protecting our ecosystems, the country also needs to strengthen measures for eradicating one of the greatest causes of deforestation: the illegal exploitation of minerals. This crime has small penalties and does not have related aggravating circumstances, such as the exploitation in national parks or protected areas, or the use of mercury or explosives in extraction activities. That is why various ministries came together in 2020 and presented the First Senate Committee with a bill to provide harsher penal, administrative and sanctionary measures against the criminal chain of exploitation, production, profiting and sale of minerals.

According to the Alluvial Gold Evidence Study (EVOA, for its Spanish acronym) by the Ministry of Mining and

Energy and the United Nations Office on Drugs and Crime (UNODC), the illicit exploitation of minerals in Colombia increased to a space of 65,000 hectares in 2018. This crime mainly affects the departments of Antioquia, Nariño, Cauca, Bolívar and Chocó. In particular, illicit activities can be found in the Puinawai Nature Reserve, between Antioquia and Córdoba, and the Farallones de Cali National Park in Valle del Cauca (see figure 7).

FIGURE 7. AREAS OF ILLEGAL EXPLOITATION OF GOLD

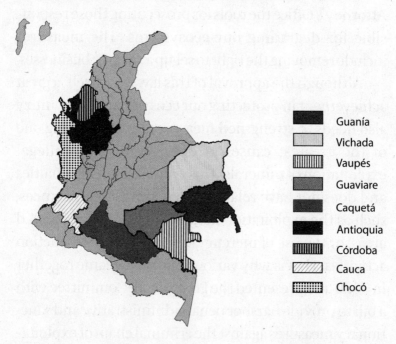

SOURCE: Ministry of Mining

As well as threatening the environment and contaminating water basins, the illegal exploitation of minerals exacerbates violence, due to the presence of organized armed groups who fight for control over the areas. Consequently, on top of suffering the impacts of the degradation of ecosystems, communities are victims of displacement, child exploitation and various criminal dynamics related to asset laundering and the funding of terrorism.

This phenomenon does not only expropriate resources belonging to all Colombians and threaten the state's strategic assets (water, the environment and biodiversity), it is also one of the main sources of funding for organized crime. In Colombia, the exploitation of minerals without a mining license or a legal mining permit is not enough to be considered a crime. Its categorization as a crime is complex, as the seriousness of the environmental damage caused by the illegal activity must be demonstrated. What's more, in protected areas where mining activity has been prohibited, high mercury contents are still being registered. It is clear, then, that prohibition alone is not enough to avoid the use of mercury in mineral exploitation, which is why it is necessary to classify the crime of possession, commercialization and use of mercury.

CHAPTER 2

Colombia, an environmental example for the world

I am proud to say that Colombia is an environmental example for the world. Our government has always tried to become a model for doing things the right way, and the environment has been a priority from day one. We are conscious of the difficult task involved in reaching the longed-for figure of zero emissions, which is why we have used all the tools at our disposal to start to build a path that will take us there.

Regional actions with a global impact

Our commitment and the results achieved with regards to the fight against deforestation, the promotion of sustainable forest management, the strengthening of communities as agents for biodiversity, among other goals, have positioned us as a key actor for signing alliances and developing joint projects with other countries and international organizations.

For example, in December 2019, we ratified the renovation of our alliance with Germany, Norway and the United Kingdom in order to continue managing, using, conserving and restoring the country's forest landscapes. With this renewed declaration of intent, Germany, Norway and the United Kingdom will contribute up to 366 million dollars, if we are able to meet the objectives agreed upon in the implementation framework.

This agreement will allow us to reach some of the transformational goals in terms of the environment and sustainability, such as a reduction by 30% of deforestation, the implementation of the Multipurpose Land Registry in 60% of the Colombian territory, a reduction in GHG emissions and the promotion of the Future Zones strategy. With this partnership, we are also seeking to meet 12 ambitious goals and various milestones for mitigating the deforestation of our natural forests, from the promotion of sustainable forest management to improving forest governance, promoting sustainable land use practices and empowering indigenous groups in their role as forest managers.

Elsewhere, we are a global example in the management of mercury and substances which are damaging to the ozone layer, and in the development of programs, with the support of international cooperation, for safeguarding tropical forests and paramos, fighting against deforestation and saving the Amazon, and reaching the goal of planting 180 million trees by August 2022. Furthermore, we are particularly committed to the task of driving sustainable growth which fosters a circular economy, in order to preserve the environment.

Colombia is part of the Minamata Convention on Mercury. The signing of this instrument took place in August 2019 and, with it, we ratified our commitment to becoming a country free of this heavy metal by 2023. Previously, with Ruling C-275 of 2019, the Constitutional Court declared Law 1892 of 2018 on the ratification of this convention constitutional.

The Minamata Convention is one of the international community's most emblematic agreements on putting an end to the use of a product which has caused a lot of pain. It takes its name from the Minamata Bay, in Japan, as a reminder of the damage caused to people's health by industrial mercury contamination in the 1950s and 1960s. The signing and implementation of this instrument strengthens actions for reducing, controlling and eliminating the use, provision and sale of this substance and products and processes which contain it. The convention also fosters knowledge development in higher education institutions, Colciencias and investigation centers to establish where the mercury is. Specifically, the aim is to eliminate around 183 tons of mercury which was dumped in soil and water in the departments of Antioquia, Chocó, Cauca and Bolívar.

Furthermore, thanks to this agreement, the country can now receive greater global cooperation and technical assistance in order to protect public health and its environmental patrimony when faced with the man-made emissions and discharges of mercury and its compounds.

Finally, and as evidence of the international support for our commitment to and leadership in managing this substance, we have been chosen to act as vice-president at the Fourth meeting of the Conference of the Parties to the Minamata Convention on Mercury, which will take place between 2021 and 2022 in two parts: virtually and physically, in Bali, Indonesia.

LET'S PROTECT THE AMAZON!

The Amazon is vital to our ecosystems and biodiversity. It contains more than 50% of the world's tropical rain-forests – around 6.7 million square kilometers – and a quarter of the planet's species. What's more, it produces 20% of Earth's fresh water.

In Colombia, the Amazon region represents around 35% of the continental territory, and that places us as the world's second-most biodiverse country per square kilo-meter, after Brazil. The sustainable protection and man-agement of its resources will allow this huge lung to be more resilient to the effects of climate change.

With the aim of tackling deforestation and its causes in the Amazon, in 2019 we signed the Leticia Pact with the governments of Brazil, Peru, Ecuador, Bolivia, Suriname, Guyana and French Guiana. This cooperation agreement, led by Colombia, has focused on sharing experiences of climate settings and designing projects aimed at adapting to climate change and the sustainable use of resources, working together with the region's communities.

The Amazon is home to 34 million people and there are more than 400 age-old communities, which is why it is vital for them to participate in decision-making for the protection, care and conservation of the natural patrimony belonging to the region.

As part of the measures taken in this regional agreement, the signatory countries have committed to providing the information required, by judicial authorities on the one hand, and border authorities on the other, with the aim of capturing those who have committed crimes against the environment in the Amazon, whether they be illegal activities relating to mining, crops, felling, the illegal trade of flora and fauna, or biopiracy. And as well as strengthening coordination mechanisms between national authorities, the countries have also agreed to immediately exchange information about trans-national criminal organizations.

These agreements make up part of a roadmap called the "Action plan", which includes 52 key actions in five thematic areas aimed at preserving and conserving the Amazon. The Leticia Pact considers the following actions:

1. Reforesting, conserving, and making sustainable use of forests and biodiversity, and promoting bioeconomy.

2. Managing knowledge and information, and creating reports.

3. Empowering women and indigenous people.

4. Achieving international financing and cooperation.

And these are the commitments:

1. Fighting against deforestation and forest degradation.

2. Establishing the *Red Amazónica de Cooperación ante Desastres Naturales* (Amazon Cooperation Network for Natural Disasters).

3. Exchanging and implementing experiences on comprehensive fire management and promoting alternatives to its use in the rural setting.

4. Promoting accelerated rehabilitation, reforestation and restoration initiatives in degraded areas.

5. Increasing the monitoring of forest cover and the climate.

6. Promoting the connectivity of prioritized ecosystems and protection figures for the conservation of biodiversity.

7. Guaranteeing the sustainable use of forests and sustainable production systems.

8. Strengthening the capacities and increasing participation of indigenous and local communities in the sustainable development of the Amazon.

In addition to the joint regional work to save the Amazon, the Ministry of Environment and Sustainable Development is heading a social program in the Amazon region in order to strengthen the conservation of forests and stop deforestation. The program is called *Visión Amazonía* (Amazon Vision) and includes various prongs: the first is focused on territorial statutes and sectoral policies; the second is aimed at the sustainable management of forests; the third drives the development of sustainable, eco-friendly production alternatives; the fourth is a monitoring system; and the fifth brings together an ethnicity focus in order to strengthen traditional indigenous communities.

Visión Amazonía's results of note include:

1.   The implementation of 131 projects for ethnic peoples and with a focus on women, with an investment of $14.47 million.

2.   Benefitting around 5,649 farming families with sustainable production systems, agricultural extension, value chains, green credits and production alliances.

3.   Allocating 1,918,088 hectares for forest development and community forest management.

4.   Registering 46,642 hectares as part of three hubs for forest development and sustainable community use.

5.   Training 600 community leaders to manage their territory, thanks to the Escuela de Selva (Jungle School) environmental education program.

6.   Accompanying five municipalities in the implementation of the School Environmental Projects (Prae, for their Spanish acronym) and Citizens' Environmental Education Projects (Proceda, for their Spanish acronym).

7.   Building the Land Use Planning Model (Motra, for its Spanish acronym), which includes the financing of

the Intermodal Transportation Plan and the Rural Electrification Plan for Caquetá.

8. Supporting around 30 municipalities in their territorial planning.

9. Promoting alternative production practices in order to maintain forests and develop sustainable production chains for meat, milk, rubber, cacao and timber.

10. Improving access to credit for the Amazon's producers, with incentives for the conservation of forests and greater access to markets.

11. Affiliating 17,200 families with the promotion of an indigenous environmental governance, using traditional practices and guaranteeing the cultural diversity of communities with self-governance and territorial and environmental governance; also, in terms of the economy and production, women and families, health and traditional medicine, local education, and strengthening indigenous languages, among other things.

12. Monitoring forest surfaces and deforestation in order to identify the impact on the biome.

13. Financing the National Forest Inventory in the Amazon in order to produce scientific information and make decisions.

Given that things have a chain reaction, the protection of the Amazon region and the fight against its deforestation have driven the development of other territorial and community strategies to make use of the region's natural, cultural and ethnic riches in a sustainable fashion. Through the National Environmental System (SINA, for its Spanish acronym), around 12,000 native trees have been planted and sustainable fishing agreements have been implemented.

Additionally, we have promoted a community allotment network in the Caquetá, Meta and Putumayo departments, in order to restore 50 hectares of forests with the planting of 17,000 trees. This project is called *Amazonía Sostenible para la Paz* (Sustainable Amazon for Peace), and has been made possible thanks to funding from the Global Environment Facility (GEF), to the tune of 9 million dollars.

This network, led by the Ministry of Environment and Sustainable Development and the United Nations Development Programme (UNDP), is an innovative model, not just because it recognizes local knowledge and the capacities of communities, but also because it offers them tools for strengthening and accessing their territorial, social and economic rights, with a resilient focus in the face of climate change. The network has a production capacity of more than a million trees per year and, in the future, it is hoped that it will contribute to the implementation of protection, restoration and sustainable production tools, in order to recover the connectivity of the Amazon's forests in more than 34,000 hectares.

WE ARE ADDING HECTARES TO PROTECTED AREAS

According to the Information System for Biodiversity (SIB, for its Spanish acronym), Colombia is home to the greatest diversity of birds and orchids in the world. It is ranked second in terms of plants, amphibians and reptiles, and fourth in terms of mammals. It contains more than 31 million hectares (18.5 million on land, and 12.8 million maritime) of protected areas across all of its natural regions. We are known as the country of butterflies, as we are home to 3,642 species, which represent 20% of all the existing species in the world. According to a recent publication by the Natural History Museum in London, 289 are endemic to the country.

This tremendous biodiversity sustains the vital ecosystems which provide water, foodstuffs and climactic regulation. However, our natural riches are under threat, which is why it is urgent that we develop key territorial protection and conservation strategies. Therefore, we have developed the strategic roadmap for the comprehensive management of protected areas in Colombia, part of the National System of Protected Areas (SINAP 2020-

2030). This is a space for inclusion, peacebuilding and new well-being opportunities. In order to promote it across the national territory and on a regional level, a public policy has been developed, with the aim of meeting the goals of protecting and conserving protected areas, social actors and all the related strategies and instruments.

In 2017, as part of the SINAP, a project for protected areas with a budget of 20 million dollars was put in place: four million comes from the Global Environment Facility, and the other 16 is made up of contributions from civil society, the World Wide Fund for Nature (WWF) and other environmental organizations. In yet another demonstration of the fact that this needs to be a collective effort, the initiative has been led by the Ministry of Environment and Sustainable Development, the Colombian National Parks Authority, the Autonomous Regional Corporation of Santander (CAS, for its Spanish acronym), the Corporation for the Sustainable Development of the La Macarena Special Management Area (Cormacarena) and the SINAP's sub-systems.

The objective of this program was to establish 550,000 hectares of protected areas in the Orinoco and north-eastern Andes within five years, with funding from the Inter-American Development Bank (IDB) and the execution of the WWF. In 2021, a year before scheduled completion, this internationally-backed project had not only met its objective, it had managed to surpass the original goal, with the protection of 650,000 hectares.

This achievement highlights the commitment of all the involved parties to continue conserving and restoring the most important areas for the health of our immense biodiversity.

Environmental education and awareness, the decisive support of the public and private sectors, as well as the hard work and support of communities, allow us to conserve what is a priority for Colombia and the world: the environment. The work to reach our environmental goals will continue in the long-term, precisely because we know that changing our reality is a matter of awareness, persistence and patience. That is why *"Herencia Colombia"* (Inheritance Colombia), a permanent funding program for conservation areas, was created, involving the participation of public and private actors in order to meet international objectives which Colombia has drawn up. These focus on the conservation and increase of protected areas and the guarantee to integrate protected areas in landscapes and sectors through the design and implementation of a long-term funding model for the SINAP.

This cooperation program is led by the Ministry of Environment and Sustainable Development, the National Parks Authority, *Patrimonio Natural*, the Gordon and Betty Moore Foundation, Conservation International, Wildlife Conservation Society and the WWF. It is also supported by GEF, *Corazón de la Amazonía* and the World Bank. Thanks to all of the representatives signing a memorandum of understanding in September of 2020, this strategy for fostering conservation through cooperation is now a reality.

With *"Herencia Colombia"*, we are looking to ensure the funding and conservation of 20 million hectares by 2040, through increased coverage and the SINAP's effective management and governance, mainly in the regions around the Andes, the Orinoco, the Amazon, the Pacific and the *Sierra Nevada of* Santa Marta, from the Ciénaga Grande wetland complex to the eastern arm of the Perijá mountain range.

This program's goals are essential to the conservation of biodiversity for future generations and for guaranteeing the well-being of communities, mitigating the effects of climate change and understanding the real responsibility we have in terms of the protection of our natural patrimony.

These efforts also come under Colombia's strong commitment to negotiating and adopting new global biodiversity goals and objectives as part of the Convention on Biological Diversity's Post-2020 Global Framework. As part of this process, Colombia has subscribed to the High Ambition Coalition for Nature and People (HAC) and the Global Ocean Alliance (GOA), which promote the conservation of 30% of the world's land mass and 30% of marine areas by 2030, as part of the Post-2020 Framework's goals. While the Framework's goals are global, under my administration, Colombia has committed to a national goal of conserving 30% of the national territory's land and marine areas by 2030, using protected areas or other effective area-based conservation measures (OECMs), a sign of Colombia's leading role in this new process, as one of the world's megadiverse countries (box 1).

BOX 1. SPECIFIC GOALS OF THE *HERENCIA COLOMBIA* PROGRAM

1. Declare 3.5 million hectares of land as new protected areas, in line with the country's commitment to the Convention on Climate Change and the widening of the capacities and strategies of SINAP.
2. Improve the management of protected areas.
3. Facilitate the conservation and sustainable use of our natural resources via a territorial governance model.

RECOVERING THE CIÉNAGA GRANDE

We celebrated World Environment Day in 2021 with some good news: that day, the Global Environment Facility's "Conservation and Sustainable Use of the Ciénaga Grande de Santa Marta" project was born, with the aim of recovering 110 kilometers of canals, protecting natural vegetation with the promotion of suitable land use, and conserving biodiversity. In order to do that, it is necessary to adopt sustainable practices in agricultural systems, with the aim of conserving forests and improving the connectivity of the tributaries.

The Ciénaga Grande de Santa Marta is a vital ecosystem, home to a huge variety of birds and wildlife, particularly in protected wetland areas with a high concentration of estuaries. The latter are vital, as they maintain the mangrove ecosystems and allow for the conservation of areas where birds can nest and fish can spawn. However, the hydrological system which guarantees the health of the Ciénaga Grande has been affected. Part of the water is used for agribusiness processes before it can reach the Ciénaga, meaning that the quality of the hydrological resource has worsened. Consequently, this project looks to promote and strengthen environmental governance and sustainable funding, as well as incorporating black, red and yellow mangrove seedlings from the National Parks Authority's nursery.

The "GEF Ciénaga Grande de Santa Marta" project will allocate 9 million dollars over five years to implementing conservation and restoration measures in mountainous, coastal and riverside forests, mangroves and natural canals. Furthermore, it aims to improve capacities in the public and private institutions which administer and govern the Ciénaga's biological and hydrological assets, and to make conservation agreements on the basin of the Fundación and Aracataca rivers. The IDB will be responsible for the funding, and its execution will depend on the Marine and Coastal Investigations Institute (Invemar, for its Spanish acronym).

As a way of reiterating Colombia's commitment to the fight against climate change, when the project was being launched in June 2021, we were joined by a group of children who were planting a mangrove, a species which is vital to environmental protection and CO_2 capture, but above all to restoring our biodiverse patrimony. Fortunately, the children and young people of the 21st century understand that protecting these ecosystems is a moral duty and their commitment to sustainability is part of the environmental revolution of younger generations which we mentioned at the start of this book.

Furthermore, this project, which promotes around 500 natural conservation contracts with communities, also seeks to recover more than 24,500 hectares in this part of the Ciénaga. An important example is the Clarín Viejo mangrove tunnel in the Vía Isla Salamanca Park, where the program's first batch of yellow mangroves has been planted. This ecological reserve has 2022's most ambitious planting goal: 185,000 trees in 300 hectares. Its recovery is a priority, given that numerous forest fires related to hunting, land invasion, woodpiling and charcoal extraction have been registered.

**FEWER SUBSTANCES THAT DEPLETE
THE OZONE LAYER**

In November 2019, Colombia had the honor of co-presiding the negotiations of the parties of the Montreal Protocol in Rome, Italy, in order to implement measures regarding CFC-11 emissions. This substance, a chloro-fluorocarbon, can be found in the insulation of some buildings, refrigerators and freezers, and is extremely harmful to the ozone layer. Although its use was banned in 2010, its effects are still contributing to the rise in the planet's temperature.

Another big problem is the use of the hydrochloro-fluorocarbons HCFC-14b and HCFC-22, other ozone-depleting substances, which can also be seen in the domestic refrigerator production processes in this country. At the end of the nineties, both substances were replaced by hydrofluorocarbons (HFC) as an alternative in the production of air conditioners, refrigeration equipment, polyurethane foams and aerosols. Currently, the use of all of these substances represents a major threat to climate stability.

Conscious of this grave situation, we took on the international commitment to promoting sustainable cold chains, which on the one hand counteract the emission of hazardous substances and, on the other hand, contribute to energy efficiency. That is why, with the financial support of the Multilateral Fund for the Implementation of the Montreal Protocol and the technical assistance of the UNDP, seven projects have been developed so that 120 small and medium companies can eliminate the use of HCFC-14b, HCFC-22 and HFC in their processes. The goal is to ensure that, by the end of 2021, these companies have adopted alternative technologies and substances which do not contribute to global warming (box 2).

BOX 2. USE OF OZONE DEPLETING SUBSTANCES IN COLOMBIA

1. Hydrochlorofluorocarbons HCFC-14b and HCFC-22: blowing agents for the injection of polyurethane foam in refrigerator doors and cabinets.
2. Hydrochlorofluorocarbons HCFC-14b: blowing agent in the fabrication of polyurethane foam for applications in: paneling; commercial refrigeration equipment; the fabrication of seats, headrests, armrests and exhausts for automobiles; as well as its use in the construction sector.

Led by the Ministry of Environment and Sustainable Development's Technical Ozone Unit (UTO, for its Spanish acronym) as part of its strategy for eliminating the use of ozone depleting substances (ODS) and meeting the commitments of the Montreal Protocol on adopting technologies to eliminate their use, this project involves thermal insulation producers as well as the air conditioning, refrigeration and fire extinguisher sectors.

As well as eliminating the use of harmful substances, it is important that the technical assistance branches of companies currently making refrigerators in Colombia develop better practices and strengthen their operational capacities in the management of refrigerants. In that regard, agreements with various companies have been established in order to guarantee good practices in the installation and maintenance of domestic refrigeration appliances, through:

• Training on the recovery of fluoro refrigerants (hydrochlorofluorocarbons, or HCFC, and hydrofluorocarbons, or HFC) and environmental management of this waste.

• Scheduling and execution of theoretical-practical workshops on the safe management of these refrigerants.

• Promoting certification of repair people and authorized workshops.

The struggle against the depleting of the ozone layer is not just limited to the elimination of this type of contaminating chemical substance. A reduction in GHG emissions is also a priority. As part of this commitment to mitigating global warming, Colombia ratified the Kigali Amendment to the Montreal Protocol, whose main objective is to reduce carbon dioxide around the world by 105 million tons, which could avoid a rise in the planet's average temperature of 0.5 degrees centigrade by the end of the century, and lead to the longed-for zero. Furthermore, thanks to this amendment, Colombia can request resources from the Multilateral Fund for the Implementation of the Montreal Protocol in order to make the transition to the use of technologies with greater energy efficiency and substances which do not harm the environment.

A CIRCULAR ECONOMY FOR SUSTAINABILITY

The national circular economy strategy that we launched in 2019 is innovative; it was the first of its kind in Latin America and has contributed to the creation of regional initiatives to drive the transition to more sustainable systems, which contribute to the post-COVID economic recovery. Its objective has been to promote the productive transformation of industrial and agricultural systems and sustainable cities in economic, environmental and social terms, taking into account factors relating to circularity, technological innovation and collaboration in new business models (see box 3).

An example of our commitment to the development of circular models is the floricultural sector, which contributed 11.5% to the rise in the country's total exports in 2021. According to the DANE (National Administrative Department of Statistics), as of May 2021, 216.7 million dollars (FOB) were declared in the export of flowers and cut stems alone. Furthermore, this sector is important to international sales because of its aim of developing processes which contribute to meeting the national goal of reducing GHG emissions by 51% by 2030.

The environmental and economic benefits are directly linked to recycling of waste products, reuse of water, and the extension of the shelf life of supplies. One of the sector's aims is to reintegrate materials into production processes, in order to drive investments with a lesser environmental impact. Additionally, the floricultural sector is fundamental to the country's sustainable economic reactivation, given that it generates green jobs which are aimed at reducing the pressure on natural capital (box 4).

Additionally, among the goals of the deal signed between the Ministry of Environment and Sustainable Development and Asocolflores (Colombian Association of Flower Exporters) are: the implementation of precision agriculture or agriculture 4.0 in order to minimize the environmental impact of crop production, the automation of irrigation systems, and data management for measuring the use of water, chemical substances, energy and the carbon footprint.

As a vital part of the "Produce while preserving, and preserve while producing" policy, the circular economy involves the cooperative work of producers, suppliers, consumers and other actors in the production and consumption systems in all the regions of Colombia. As well as developing more efficient processes for managing materials and waste, it seeks to generate a positive change in the lifestyles of inhabitants (see box 5).

Aware of the importance of offering training in a circular economy, and of the need for those involved in processes which manage water, energy and other natural resources to learn about models of efficient development, waste reuse, and sustainable consumption, an alliance has been made between the National Learning Service (SENA, for its Spanish acronym), the Ministry of Environment and Sustainable Development and the

Green Employment in the Circular Economy Program (Prevec, for its Spanish acronym), which has allowed 880 people from across the country's regions to train virtually on developing processes and projects which make use of recyclable waste. In March 2021, the first 320 students gained their qualification.

BOX 5. MAIN ACHIEVEMENTS OF THE CIRCULAR ECONOMY STRATEGY PRESENTED AT THE DAVOS WORLD ECONOMIC FORUM 2020

1. Fifty public and private actors signed the national pact.
2. The comprehensive management of pests using biological control and materials.
3. More than 3,000 people attended 19 regional teaching workshops on circular economy, with the presentation of more than 80 successful initiatives.
4. More than 230 trade unions, academic institutions, mayor's offices, local governments, NGOs, recycling organizations and civil society organizations signed 16 regional pacts.
5. More than 450 people committed to circular economy strategies in the hydrocarbon, agricultural and residential utilities sectors.
6. The training benefitted more than 11,000 people.
7. The implementation of 15 workshops, by sector, with more than 250 attendees, led to 29 agreed-upon objectives and 43 defined actions.

8. The creation of the Circular Economy Information System (SIEC, for its Spanish acronym).
9. Two sessions of the Circular Economy Information Roundtable, with more than 100 participants.
10. The first edition of the training program for central and regional government public servants in Bogotá and Cundinamarca.
11. Including the circular economy in inter-ministerial agendas and the signing of sector agreements to consolidate sustainable production sectors.
12. Development of seven successful initiatives on sources and use of energy, and twelve on water cycles.
13. Agreement with Ecopetrol on better management of type Y9 hazardous waste, which include mixtures and emulsions of waste oils and water, and hydrocarbons and water.

As well as these training courses, virtual circular economy days have been carried out for the education sector, with the support of the Ministries of Education and Science, Technology and Innovation. These training days have been key to raising awareness of case studies in the regions and identifying new lines which permit technological development and innovation, the updating of study programs, and the identification of tools for overcoming financial, social or administrative gaps in the implementation of the circular economy.

Apart from education, another key element of circular economy processes is inclusion. That is why we are convinced that the recycling associations and their members are vital to the protection of the environment. Thanks to the classification of waste by recyclers, waste which can be reused does not end up on landfill sites, and that is a significant step towards a circular economy, as it contributes to meeting the Sustainable Development Goals (SDGs).

Now, in order for recyclers to be able to carry out their job properly, it is vital that all of us, at home and in our companies, use the color-coded waste classification system. In this process of halting environmental deterioration and guaranteeing our children and grandchildren a clean, inhabitable planet, we need to be aware that what we do not only affects ourselves, but it also affects our community, our country and our planet.

Finally, it is important to remember that the waste management policy generates various environmental, social and economic benefits, as it targets the strengthening of recycling instruments, a reduction in the exploitation of natural resources, income generation for families, and the development of more competitive processes with lower costs in production sectors. Taken together, all of these actions will allow for the better management of the 32,294 daily tons of waste which are produced on average across the national territory. With this in mind, it is worth highlighting that, according to the Ombudsman for Public Utilities, in 2018 recyclers reincorporated around 970,000 tons of waste into the production cycle, and in 2019 recycling rose to 1.4 million tons.

CLEAN TRANSPORTATION:
AN ISSUE FOR EVERYONE ON THE PLANET

Without doubt, improving transportation in cities does not just mean less traffic on the roads, it also has a much more important short- and long-term impact: improving the air that we all breathe and, in the process, reducing the environmental damages affecting the planet and improving our health. In 2018, the costs of respiratory health associated to the quality of air we breathe rose to $3.24 million, and it is estimated that nearly 8 million people died from related causes. That is to say that, in one year, almost the same amount of people as those living in Bogotá died. Is that not another reason for us to give our all to care for the environment?

The transport sector consumes 37.6% of the country's energy, and 96.5% of that energy is made up of the consumption of liquid fuels. We know that the change in thinking that we have been proposing, and taking measures in that respect, is a process that will take time, which is why the government has been focused on accelerating the electric transition on every level. One of the most effective measures, with which we have seen significant progress, is the consolidation of electric transport, given that nearly 80% of the poor quality air is produced by means of transport, both public and private. Our objective is the same as all countries committed to the environment: zero carbon emissions.

With this in mind, we proposed the ambitious goal of registering, by 2022, 6,600 electric vehicles in the National Transportation Register (RUNT, for its Spanish acronym), and facilitating the conditions for this number to reach 600,000 by 2030. We are making good progress with this goal, and by August 2021, we already had 4,840 vehicles registered (see figure 8).

Figure 8. Registered electric vehicles in Colombia (as of August 2021)

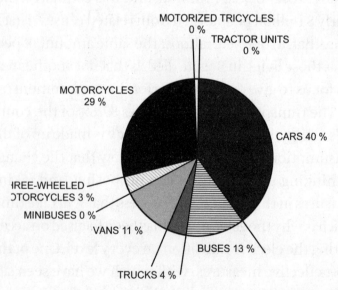

MOTORIZED TRICYCLES 0 %

TRACTOR UNITS 0 %

MOTORCYCLES 29 %

CARS 40 %

ÌREE-WHEELED ÌTORCYCLES 3 %

MINIBUSES 0 %

VANS 11 %

BUSES 13 %

TRUCKS 4 %

Source: RUNT (2021).

But the good news is not just that we have reached almost 5,000 electric cars, but also that the number of hybrid cars registered in the country has reached 15,000. These figures tell us that the number of electric vehicles on the roads has doubled since 2018, and that is very significant in terms of caring for the environment.

According to figures from Colombia's National Inventory of Greenhouse Gases, for which the IDEAM is responsible, the transportation sector is responsible for 12% of the country's emissions, the equivalent of 28 million tons of carbon dioxide. In the Paris Climate Agreement, Colombia committed to reducing its GHGs by 51% by 2030, which is why all sectors need to share this mission. Transport is key, as it affects all citizens indiscriminately: all of us, no matter where we live or what our job is, have to go out onto the streets and move from one place to another, and if we do that conscientiously, we will progress more quickly towards this goal.

As part of all of the decisions we make to help the environment, we must also consider the effect of transportation. There are various ways to become part of this plan to emit less than half of the gases we emit today by 2030. Such as? Looking for alternative means of transport which do not contaminate, like bicycles, or car sharing with people taking the same route, for example. The implementation of good practices and the adoption of new technologies and comprehensive energy management systems could represent savings of between 5% and 50% in consumption.

The following five fields are those in which we have focused our efforts to turn transportation in the country into an ally in our dream of managing, hopefully one day not too far from now, to reduce GHG emissions to zero:

1. Promoting electric vehicles: we have provided a series of facilitating conditions and economic and technical incentives, which have allowed us to reach a figure of almost 5,000 electric vehicles on our roads. But given that the idea is that all of us, as a country, feel like we are part of the effort, public transportation is key, and the goal is to have 1,160 electric vehicles and 1,361 natural gas vehicles in 2021.

2. Modernizing the cargo fleet: we want transporters to be able to move around in more modern vehicles, which do not simply offer greater efficiency and competitiveness, but which also help us to reduce gas emissions. Furthermore, we have been working on the National Electric Transportation Strategy in order to give an additional impetus to eco-friendly automobiles. This strategy is an action plan aimed at creating a regulatory and policy framework which will help us fulfill what we signed at the Paris Agreement and, in the long-term, achieve zero emissions.

With such a big goal, we need to think big, which is why the strategy does not just consider solutions for road travel; it also implements actions for rail and water transport, including the infrastructure needed for their operation. Among the technologies available are electric, natural gas, hydrogen, hybrid, diesel, and low-sulfur gasoline vehicles.

3. Entirely electric fleet for the mass transport system: the transport systems which are co-financed by the state are beginning to introduce vehicles with zero-emissions or very low emissions, which makes us the Latin American country with the largest electric public transport fleet. And Bogotá, our capital, will become the city with the most electric public transport vehicles in the region.

By the end of 2021, Colombia will have 1,160 electric buses, while Mexico has 369, Chile has 776 and Brazil has 349. This is yet another example of the good we are doing for the planet.

4. Commitment to co-financing new rail projects: convinced that this is an excellent form of transport for passengers and cargo, the government has co-financed various projects which seek to improve the quality of life of citizens and improve the air we all breathe. These projects include the first line of

Bogotá's metro system, the RegioTram de Occidente (Cundinamarca) and Medellín's light rail.

Reaching zero emissions requires the use of technology, but also constant investment in order to apply it and think outside the box. Improving the quality of public transportation will ensure it is used more, which will reduce the circulation of a large amount of private vehicles. This will not only bring us better air, but a better transport experience and the change from an individual thinking to a collective conscience which seeks big solutions for our planet.

5.   Regulation: in order to create the facilitating conditions for each of these projects, it is key that we release a series of regulations. For example, the National Electric Transportation Strategy, launched in 2019, promotes, through the use of public policies, the necessary regulatory, economic, technical and territorial planning instruments. Without this, we would not be able carry out everything proposed in the Development Plan, whose ultimate goal is to allow us to live in a country, and planet, with zero GHG emissions, and enjoy all that comes with that.

Now, it is vital to think about this transition in a viable and safe way, which is why the regulation is so relevant to the project for achieving zero emissions. Renewing the public transportation fleet is a responsibility to the environment and also to the citizens who use it: we must guarantee that the vehicles meet security conditions in order to avoid accidents (box 6).

BOX 6. SOME KEY REGULATIONS RELATED TO TRANSPORTATION

1. Law 1964 of 2019 stipulated that the tax on electric vehicles cannot be more than 1% of the commercial value of the vehicle, and that they should receive discounts on the SOAT (obligatory auto insurance) and be exempt from vehicular restrictions.
2. The Modernization Program Resolution offers additional incentives if new vehicles are low or zero-emissions (electric, hybrid or natural gas).
3. The Ministry of Mining and Energy emitted Resolution 40405 of 2020, which regulates the technical conditions for fossil fuel refilling stations, so that they increase the electric energy offering for electric vehicles.
4. Decree 2051 of 2019 established a duty tax of 0% for electric vehicles and 5% for natural gas vehicles.
5. Tax statutes established a VAT of 5% for electric vehicles.
6. Through the Rational and Efficient Use of Energy Program, people can access an exemption from VAT payments for electric and natural gas vehicles.

Finally, we must not forget that this is a cross-cutting theme which involves us all. For the government's part, Law 697 of 2001 declared the rational and efficient use of energy a matter of social, public and national interest, fundamental to ensuring a full and appropriate supply of energy, the competitiveness of the Colombian economy, consumer protection and the promotion of the use of non-conventional energy sources in a way which is sustainable with the environment and natural resources.

Furthermore, let us remember that the issue of clean transportation is vital to our zero emissions goal, as it is our current means of transport which generate such high quantities of GHGs due to the use of fossil fuels, and the more we do to reduce these, the better the quality of air, health and well-being that we can guarantee future generations. So, in order to reach excellent air quality standards, transportation and public spaces must center on the collective, because the solution is in everybody's hands and it is a global responsibility.

ENERGY TRANSITION

Energy transition is an important topic for the world, and part of the fight against climate change. It relies on current and future generations migrating towards a more competitive, sustainable, efficient and resilient energy system, making use of non-conventional, renewable energy and adopting new technologies that can eliminate the electricity access gaps, through business models and new technologies which accelerate the universalization of electric energy and fuel gas. It also relies on those generations taking control of the fight against climate change, as they have been doing, prioritizing sustainable transportation with the mass introduction of low- or zero-emission fuels, the use of hybrid or electric vehicles, and energy efficiency policies in all sectors.

Although Colombia has made significant progress over the last three years, especially in the design of a competitive regulatory framework, which is attractive to private investment, it still has plenty of potential to take this transition further. We have two of the necessary conditions to achieve this, but it is worth reminding ourselves that they are not enough. Firstly, our geographical location and topography allow us to be a world power in this respect; for example, Colombia is the sixth-highest ranked country in the world in terms of renewable hydraulic resources, with 2,360 km^2 of water per year, surpassed only by Brazil, the United States, Canada, Russia and China. What do those countries have in common that we do not have? Much larger land masses. Equally, we have world-class wind and solar resources, with a comparative advantage over other countries, given that our location close to the equator and lack of seasons means that these resources are more stable and predictable. For example, the La Guajira department alone has a coastal and inland wind power potential of 25 gigawatts (GW), greater than the country's entire current installed capacity, and initial reports of the offshore potential indicate that this could be somewhere between 10 and 37 GW. Finally, solar radiation in Colombia is well above the global average, at 4.5 kWh per square meter.

Secondly, respect for private property and foreign investment, as well as our legal and institutional stability, have given important national and international companies the confidence in our policies and regulatory frameworks to make substantial, long-term investments in the country.

While we do benefit from two important conditions, it is important that we, as a country, commit to caring for our resources, by being more conscious with our consumption and routines, and by each of us spreading this message. Planet Earth is heating up at an unimaginable speed and stopping that is in our hands, so that our children and grandchildren have an inhabitable place in years to come.

Furthermore, it is important to keep creating and developing public policies which allow the private sector to speed up this transition process. For example, Law 697 of 2001 fosters the rational and efficient use of energy, and promotes the use of alternative energy sources. This law defined, for the first time, non-conventional energy sources as those available on a global scale which are environmentally sustainable, but were not used or were used sparingly in this country.

For its part, Law 1715 of 2014 was the first regulatory mandate which provided direct fiscal or regulatory benefits to non-conventional energy sources. In the National Development Plan (PND, for its Spanish acronym), approved in Law 1955 of 2019, we made important modifications to Law 1715, introducing incentives and specific measures for accelerating the incorporation of non-conventional, renewable energy and energy efficiency. It is worth highlighting three important measures. The first was extending the deadline, from 5 to 15 years, for using the incentive of a 50% reduction for investments in generator equipment for non-conventional, renewable energy and energy efficiency in income tax calculations. Secondly, in order to eliminate unnecessary red tape and democratize the use of solar power systems, we introduced the automatic VAT exclusion for solar panel, inverter and solar charge controller purchases. This change signified an important efficiency improvement, as Law 1715 previously only offered such an exemption with a prior, lengthy procedure, as part of which it was necessary to indicate ahead of time what specific project these goods would be used for. Finally, it included a stipulation that 10% of the energy sold to final users by energy companies should come from non-conventional, renewable sources.

We also included important incentives for capital-intensive industries, such as energy, in Law 1943 of 2018 – Law of Growth or Funding -, which was processed towards the end of 2018. Two important landmarks of this law were: gradually reducing corporate income tax and ensuring that the entirety of the VAT paid on the acquisition or creation of real, fixed assets would be deductible from the income tax, as well as 50% of the industry and commerce tax paid by businesses.

In July 2021, we approved Law 2099 on Energy Transition, which consolidates the regulatory framework for non-conventional, renewable energies and new technologies. This expanded on Law 1715's objective by including large-scale energy storage, intelligent measuring, green and blue hydrogen, carbon capture and storage, geothermal energy and offshore wind energy. Furthermore, fiscal incentives were improved and extended to these new sources and technologies. Finally, the Energy Transition Law included measures for accelerating the closing of electricity access gaps and a migration to a cleaner transport system, using low and zero-emission fuels.

As part of the regulatory framework and public policy innovation for energy transition, we developed an unprecedented bidding program for Colombia. This marked the entry point for non-conventional, renewable energy projects on a large-scale. After a failed attempt in February 2019, the first non-conventional, renewable energy auction in the country took place successfully in October of the same year, in which 1,365 megawatts were awarded, a little more than 45 times the installed capacity for solar and wind power we had in August 2018. This was the first double-sided renewable energy auction in the world, which means that both energy suppliers and buyers made bids on price and quantity. The auction also managed to introduce the start of a long-term contract culture (15 years in the case of auctioned products), which was practically non-existent in Colombia. And, perhaps most importantly, the auction brought about historically low prices, around 35% lower than the prices of the energy contracts that were being agreed at the time of the auction.

Due to the good reception of these mechanisms, the Ministry of Mining and Energy is in the process of carrying out another renewable energy auction and, after the process of bid collecting and market clearing in September 2021, there were already 47 buyers, double the amount registered in 2019, and 22 suppliers represented in 38 solar and wind projects.

Additionally, in June 2021, we carried out the first auction in Latin America for utility-scale battery storage. This project will take place in the Atlántico department, with a storage capacity of 45 MW. This represents a milestone, bringing together the expansion needs of the energy generation sector, the complementary services for the transmission and distribution networks, and backing for non-conventional, renewable energies.

Four years ago we made an important and clear diagnosis of the path we were on: as a country, we needed to design and implement public policies and regulatory measures which would facilitate the path towards making the most of our potential for non-conventional, renewable energy and speed up the objectives we had planned for energy transition.

The legacy we are leaving behind in this regard involves the following:

- Non-conventional, renewable energy sources: we have increased the country's installed capacity for non-conventional, renewable energy projects by more than 11 times, going from having less than 30 MW in 2018 to more than 320 MW by August 2021. Currently, the country has 15 large-scale wind farms, with an installed capacity of 236 MW, and more than 1,500 small projects for subsistence or small and medium-scale distribution, located across the country with an installed capacity of 87 MW. Additionally, we close out 2021 with more than 560 MW, having multiplied the installed capacity we had in August 2018 by 20. By the end of this government's term, there will be more than 1,600 MW of installed capacity in non-conventional, renewable energy projects and, including the projects set to start operations before December 31, 2022, this number will be more than 2,200 MW, an increase of more than 70 times the installed capacity of 2018.

- Closing electricity access gaps: our goal is universal access. By the end of 2021, more than 70,000 families will have access to electricity for the first time and, by the end of 2022, we hope this number will rise to 110,000 new homes. We all have a duty, but we all have rights too.

• Energy transformation mission: more than 20 national and international experts made detailed recommendations on modernizing the electricity sector. This mission involved various entities and agents from the energy sector, which fostered discussions and opinion-sharing, resulting in a teamwork-built roadmap.

• Intelligent measurement: as I have mentioned, this is a project for and by everyone, which is why the final consumer must have access to all the information in order to make informed decisions and so that all of these proposals are carried out correctly. Making the necessary tools and information available to consumers so that they can change their routines is the responsibility of the public and private sector, and it is each of our responsibility to be informed and make changes.

• Hydrogen: The Ministry of Mining and Energy created a roadmap for hydrogen in Colombia, with the aim of plotting the path to implementing this energy source in the country's economy, contributing to the objectives of the Paris Agreement 2015 and the national government's commitment to carbon neutrality by 2050. Colombia possesses exceptional conditions for developing low emission hydrogen thanks to the richness of its natural resources and its special geographic location. The country is a competitive, world-class producer, with a production potential of between 1 GW and 3 GW of electrolytic hydrogen and 50 kT of blue hydrogen by 2030; this will speed up the rollout of non-conventional, renewable energy sources and the coal industry's transition to cleaner technologies, which will reduce between 2.5 and 3 MTCO2e in the 2020s and 2030s. In terms of local demand and the export potential, there are opportunities in the short-term for transportation applications and use in industries such as refineries and fertilizer production. In the medium to long-term, new applications will be developed, which will promote the international trading of hydrogen, a market in which Colombia is positioned as one of the region's leading exporters, setting up new value chains with the creation of 15,000 high quality jobs and the mobilization of 5.5 billion dollars by 2030.

• Climate change: According to the World Energy Outlook 2020, the world emits 0.59 MTCO2e per GWh, but Colombia is well below this average, with 0.16 MTCO2e per GWh generated in 2019. This means that we are one of the world's cleanest countries. We are on the right path, and we have various tools for meeting the long and medium-term goals. That is why I decided to write this book: we should be proud of what we have achieved as a country and continue to be committed to change for our environment.

Feeling proud is the greatest reward. The world recognizes our leading role in terms of the environment and energy transition. According to the World Economic Forum, Colombia is the country which has made the greatest progress towards energy transition in Latin America: it rose nine positions in the Energy Transition Index, moving from 34th to 25th place. After Uruguay (11), Colombia is the second country from Latin America and the Caribbean to appear on the list, surpassing countries like Chile and Costa Rica. Equally, the country rose 14 positions in the World Energy Council's Energy Sustainability Index, moving from 49th to 35th place, and occupying the sixth highest spot among Latin American and Caribbean countries.

Furthermore, the United Nations selected us, alongside Denmark, Brazil, Germany, Spain, India and the United Kingdom, as one of the seven leading countries in energy transition.

I repeat, we are on the right path, but it is not time to give up.

What makes us important in the global environmental setting?

Colombia is one of the 40 most vulnerable countries to the effects of climate change. Therefore, protecting the natural riches of our territories, by meeting environmental goals, is a priority for the country. Our agenda for promoting sustainable development has been recognized by various countries and organizations for its urgent and ambitious nature, as it not only includes carbon neutrality by 2050, but also a reduction of deforestation to 0% and GHG emissions by 51% by 2030.

But these are not promises, they are objectives which nourish the actions we are already carrying out. With our commitment to the Paris Agreement, Colombia will stop emitting 176.8 million tons of GHGs into the atmosphere by 2030. Elsewhere, Colombia is making progress in energy transition, making decisions to meet the goal of going from 0.5% of use of non-conventional, renewable energies in 2018 to 14% by August 2022. Furthermore, the country is also promoting the use of cleaner transportation, with the largest urban electric transport fleet in Latin America and the Caribbean.

In terms of deforestation, the goal is to plant 180 million trees by August 2022. As of October 2021, 70,134,820 trees had been planted in 28 departments, incorporating more than 250 native species into the ecosystems. This forest regeneration makes up part of a collection of initiatives, including the Leticia Pact to recover the Amazon, the circular economy policy based on "Produce while preserving, and preserve while producing", and the creation of nature-based solutions, such as payments for environmental services and nature conservation contracts.

We Colombians have done our job so well that the international relevance of Colombia in environmental terms has been recognized with its joining of the Organization for Economic Co-operation and Development (OECD). For example, the national policies on risk management associated with the use of chemical substances and the comprehensive management of solid waste were decisive to the approval of the evaluation by 23 committees in 2018.

As well as these two commitments, the country has made progress with the Extended Producer Responsibility of packaging and containers, which makes use of used tires and hazardous waste. This includes commonly-used products and supplies, such as used oil, batteries, lead batteries, light bulbs, computers and electronic devices, expired medicine and pesticide containers.

In the same way, with its leading circular economy strategy, Colombia is looking to make use of more than 200,000 tons of containers and packaging by the end of 2021. The Ministry of Environment and Sustainable Development's Resolution 1342 of December 2020 put into effect collective and individual environmental management plans for this waste, which compels waste management companies to meet the technical or legal requirements of the relevant regional or local environmental authority. Furthermore, they now have more tools for measuring and reporting their environmental management plans (box 7).

BOX 7. WHAT ENVIRONMENTAL MANAGEMENT PLANS FOR USED CONTAINERS AND PACKAGING INCLUDE AND WHAT THEY DO NOT INCLUDE

- They do not include containers and packaging with dangerous waste, with wood and natural fibers or textiles (except paper and cardboard), and pharmaceuticals and medication packaging.
- They include the recovery of containers and packaging, using energy valuation, co-processing and/or recycling.
- They include containers with layers of different materials, and returnable bottles.
- They include a returnability efficiency measure to determine the amount of containers and packets which do not make it into the producer's return cycle.

These advancements are just a sample of the impact of government policies and citizens who are more conscious regarding caring for our ecosystems. With more than 63,303 registered species and almost 31 million protected hectares, our commitment to the preservation of land and forest reserves is crucial to guaranteeing the lives of bird and orchid species, plants, amphibians, butterflies, freshwater fish, palm trees, reptiles and mammals. The conservation of our strategic ecosystems guarantees the supply of essential environmental goods and services for the country's development. It also protects our cultural patrimony, food production chains and our health.

Now, in terms of the international effort to stop the illegal trade of fauna, flora and their by-products, Colombia is a model, thanks to its joint work on the borders with Peru and Ecuador. These bi-national prevention and forest resource management networks are key to counteracting one of the main threats to the region's biodiversity and act as an example of teamwork aimed at a common goal.

In 2020, the national environmental authorities, investigation institutes, the District Attorney's Office, the army and the National Police Force seized 19,580 animal species and 202,255 plant species. This is on top of the 114,000 species, including reptiles, birds and mammals, which were recovered between 2010 and 2019. As well as seizing illegally-trafficked species, an infrastructure for these species has been consolidated. Currently, Colombia has 12 temporary shelters, 17 centers for the attention to and assessment of wildlife (CAVS, for their Spanish acronym) and 12 centers for attention, assessment and rehabilitation (CAVR, for their Spanish acronym).

Furthermore, the penalties for illegal wildlife trade have been getting heavier over the years. The Penal Code establishes sentences of between 32 and 90 months in jail, and fines of up to 15,000 minimum salaries for those who commit this crime. The Police Code also includes corrective measures.

The road ahead

Although we have undertaken numerous actions to counteract the degradation of our ecosystems and mitigate the impact of climate change, we know it is still not enough. There remains a long road ahead in order to eliminate the causes and agents of deforestation in our forests, which are directly related to the misappropriation and seizure of land, unsustainable extensive livestock breeding practices, the unplanned development of transport infrastructure, the illicit extraction of minerals and timber, the extension of the agricultural frontier in prohibited areas, and illegal crops.

According to the Forest and Carbon Monitoring System (SMByC, for its Spanish acronym) and IDEAM, in 2020, 171,685 hectares of forest were lost, and deforestation rose by 8% compared with 2019. The results of our strategy are already beginning to show in the tracking figures: in the first quarter of 2021, we have seen a reduction of around 30% in deforestation, compared with the results of the first quarter of 2020. The deforested area was around 41,600 ha, while in the first quarter of 2020 this figure was 62,200 ha. A similar situation can be seen in the second quarter of the year, with an accumulative reduction on the first six months of 2021 of 34%, compared with the first six months of 2020. The greatest reductions can be seen in Caquetá.

In 2017, the country saw the highest spike in the last 20 years, with 219,552 deforested hectares. However, we have achieved an accumulative reduction of around 22%. In 2018, we saw a reduction of 19%, in 2019, a reduction of 10%, and although 2020 saw an increase of 8%, this is already being counteracted successfully. Our goal is zero deforestation by 2030 (see box 8).

BOX 8. STRATEGIES THE GOVERNMENT IS IMPLEMENTING IN ORDER TO FIGHT AGAINST DEFORESTATION

1. Legislation: as well as the deforestation CONPES and the Environmental Crimes Law, Ruling 690 of 2021 seeks to regulate the sustainable management of wild flora and non-timber-yielding forest products.
2. Controlling illegality: control of 15,200 hectares of forest has been taken back as a result of 11 Artemisa Campaign operations.
3. Social investment: payments for environmental services have helped protect more than 115,000 hectares of natural ecosystems. Across the country, 2,581 green

Continues on the next page

businesses, nature conservation contracts and environmental training schools have also been strengthened.

4. Fight against climate change: the goal is to reduce GHGs by 51% by 2030.

5. Planting trees: with the help of communities, environmental authorities and the public and private sector, 70 million trees have been planted. The aim is to reach 125 million by the end of 2021 and 180 million by 2022.

Elsewhere, the national environmental agenda, focused on energy transition, clean transportation, the planting of trees, the circular economy and carbon neutrality, has the support of international partners for its implementation. We are not alone in the project to save our biodiversity, fight against deforestation, preserve our hydraulic resources and counteract forest fires. With knowledge transfer from successful cases in Denmark and France, we will have more tools for strengthening institutions, technological development, and the regulation and implementation of sustainable projects in the national territory. For example, the generation of electric energy through non-conventional, renewable sources such as solar and wind power in Barranquilla and the Atlántico department can become a reality. It will also be possible to develop green urban planning in Bogotá and Medellín.

As well as support for the implementation of the agenda to mitigate climate change, we have managed to attain 158 million dollars in financial contributions from Germany, Norway, Switzerland, Sweden, the United Kingdom, the European Union, the United Nations and multilateral banking. Similarly, the various alliances have been strengthened thanks to the results of the innovative and resilient projects taking place to save the Amazon, to implement sustainable development models for food security and agroforestry, to deal with environmental crimes, and to promote sustainable production alternatives and a circular economy which protects forests and improves the social, economic and well-being conditions of communities, among other actions.

A DEBT TO THE PARAMOS
Thanks to international cooperation, Colombia has been able to allocate one of the largest budgets in its history to protecting and saving the paramos. Their conservation is vital in the fight against climate change, given that they contribute to capturing carbon and regulating the process of global warming. However, they are very vulnerable ecosystems with slow growth, and the degradation of their soil as a result of fires and land invasion, as well as the loss of their vegetation, threaten not only the survival of flora and fauna, but also the springing of tributaries and water provision (see figure 9).

FIGURE 9. A DEBT TO THE PARAMOS

SOURCE: Ministry of Environment and Sustainable Development (2021).

Colombia is a country of paramos and we are indebted to them. We must remember that half of the paramos on the planet can be found in our territory, stretching over 3 million hectares. The largest in the world is the paramo complex of Cruz Verde-Sumapaz, covering around 333,420 hectares of flora, fauna and unique landscapes (see figure 10).

FIGURE 10. PARAMOS IN COLOMBIA

Half of the planet's paramos are found in our territories, spread across 3 million hectares

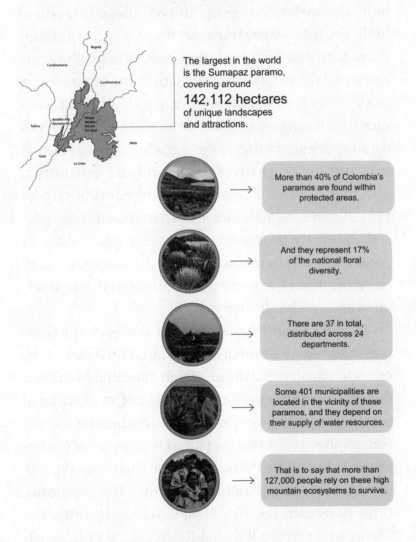

The largest in the world is the Sumapaz paramo, covering around

142,112 hectares
of unique landscapes and attractions.

More than 40% of Colombia's paramos are found within protected areas.

And they represent 17% of the national floral diversity.

There are 37 in total, distributed across 24 departments.

Some 401 municipalities are located in the vicinity of these paramos, and they depend on their supply of water resources.

That is to say that more than 127,000 people rely on these high mountain ecosystems to survive.

SOURCE: Ministry of Environment and Sustainable Development (2021).

145

We have 37 paramos, distributed across 24 departments. Nearly 401 municipalities can be found in their vicinity, and they depend on their water supply. That means that more than 3.4 million people directly depend on these high altitude ecosystems, so it is vital to find and strengthen sustainable solutions that allow for economic and social development at the same time as protecting biodiversity. For example, encouraging low impact activities which can provide economic and food security to communities, whether they be gradual conversion and substitution alternatives to high impact agricultural activities, or a gradual contribution to substitution processes for mining activities in the paramos. It is also possible to create programs and projects which directly conserve ecosystems and allow for the proper management of socio-environmental conflicts, ecosystem services and agrobiodiversity.

In order to find these solutions alongside the communities, we have the support of the GEF (Global Environment Facility) Portfolio, which allocated 15 million dollars of resources to protecting 16 of the 37 national paramos over five years. So, as of the first quarter of 2021, conservation projects in the paramo complexes of Chiles-Cumbal, La Cocha-Patascoy, Sotará, Guanacas-Puracé-Coconucos, Nevado del Huila-Moras, Las Hermosas, Chili-Barragán, Los Nevados, Cruz Verde-Sumapaz, Chingaza, Guerrero, Rabanal-Río Bogotá, Tota-Bijagual-

Mamapacha, Pisba, Cocuy and Santurbán-Berlín have been implemented (see figure 11).

FIGURE 11. CONSERVATION PROJECTS

SOURCE: Ministry of Environment and Sustainable Development (2021).

This project will benefit paramos located in Nariño, Cauca, Tolima, Risaralda, Caldas, Huila, Cundinamarca, Meta, Boyacá, Arauca and Norte de Santander, the equivalent of nearly half of our entire paramo system. Of these resources, 6 million dollars are driving the "Paramos for life" project, which protects and conserves more than 379,000 hectares of the Santurbán, Pisba, Puracé and Los Nevados paramos. Another 4,000 hectares will be set aside exclusively for the development of restoration processes, integrated systems and biodiversity. As part of these processes, 560 members of local communities will participate in the generation of alternatives to substitute mining and agricultural activities in high mountain areas. They will also promote ecotourism and agro-tourism projects, and sustainable agriculture with native species.

As well as developing sustainable projects, it is vital to mitigate the potential seats of fires which can destroy ecosystem services and wildlife corridors. The fire registered in February 2021, near the Santurbán paramo, is a case of damage to biodiversity which should not be repeated. As a result of the blaze, the water cycle was altered by changes in air quality, and the land was exposed to erosion due to changes in the fertility of the soil and the nutrient cycle. The affected area is a strategic ecosystem within the wildlife corridor of the Andean condor (*Vultur gryphus*) and other species.

The path to saving the paramos will involve a joint effort between communities, municipal governments and corporations in order to prevent fires and understand that controlled burning and open fires are not permitted in protected areas. As I have already repeated on numerous occasions, conserving and recovering our diversity requires everybody's commitment.

THE FIGHT AGAINST FOREST FIRES

Since March 2021, Colombia and the countries with whom we share the Amazon have had a Protocol for the Management of Forest Fires. Thanks to this new tool, there are now guarantees for the development of coordinated actions for controlling fires, if these exceed the capacities of national authorities. Unfortunately, fires continue to occur as a result of human actions, as well as lack of rain and high temperatures. That is why hotspots have been monitored since February 2021 to allow for quick reactions and avoid the burning of forests, flora and fauna. However, we need to reinforce all possible actions to control the spread of fire.

With the sum of efforts of the Leticia Pact signatories, it will be possible to react quickly and mobilize international teams to put out fires and minimize their impact on the ecosystems, sources of oxygen and animal and plant species. Yolanda González, the first woman to direct IDEAM, explains that this roadmap will "allow us to act in a coordinated fashion with environmental entities, both in Colombia and in the countries in the Amazon basin who are committed to better controlling fires and their effects on the territory and communities" (MinAmbiente, 2021z). However, and in the same way as with all projects to preserve our ecosystems, a reduction in forest fires will not be possible without the work of the communities. Therefore, joint work models between local authorities and inhabitants are crucial.

For example, in the municipality of Riosucio (Caldas), they have created and promoted a joint work model in order to mitigate forest fires. Twenty-four years ago, the local fire brigade and the indigenous leaders agreed to create an Indigenous Volunteer Fire Brigade, and there are currently no registered forest fires in the municipality. As a result, the model has been replicated in 14 areas across the national territory. As well as reducing the number of forest fires to zero, it has accelerated the process of reforestation of native species and species under threat of extinction in areas where livestock rearing formerly took place.

Elsewhere, in the San Andrés and Providencia archipelago, a similar model was put in place in February 2021, with the participation of islanders. The task of preventing fires on the islands is led by the forest fire lookouts, who aim to mitigate the burning of vegetable matter. This, combined with high temperatures and wind, represents a threat to the preservation of the dry forests and the islands' land and marine ecosystems.

This initiative, launched jointly with the IDEAM, National Parks Authority, Coralina, the Providencia Mayor's Office, the fire brigade and armed forces, as well as other local contributors and island locals, makes up part of the "Payments for environmental services" program, which I will expand on in the following chapter.

This local and regional work has been complemented by a national initiative to contribute to a reduction in the areas affected by fires in Colombia. It is a recurring phenomenon in a large part of the country, especially during prolonged dry spells. The "Project for the tracking, monitoring and management of forest fires in Colombia" initiative was created by the Ministries of the Environment and the Interior, and the Colombian National Firefighters' Administration.

This project, which proposes a strengthening of institutional capacities for the tracking, monitoring and management of forest fires, will act on four fronts: the first will involve air support and the management of forest fires in strategic ecosystems, prioritizing national parks; the second will strengthen the forest fire control station network in the Amazon by building new stations; the third will update the means of communication used by the entities involved in the control of forest fires; and the fourth will create Colombia's forest lookout group.

HOW DO WE REDUCE THE CONSUMPTION OF SINGLE-USE PLASTICS?

The consumption of single-use plastic bags in Colombia has reduced by almost 70% between 2015 and 2021, but we still need to deal with the 30% that continues to make its way to the market. This implies radically changing our consumption habits and strengthening our environmental awareness of the impact of plastic waste and micro-plastics on the ecosystems. In 2015 alone, more than a billion plastic bags were used in the country's shops. In 2021, the official figure was 315 million bags.

Among the national strategies for promoting the reuse, recycling and circular economy of plastic waste, the national plan for managing single-use plastics stands out. This plan is key to reducing the impact of climate change, as it prioritizes the reuse of waste and avoids it further contaminating our ecosystems.

The country has a long-term commitment to reducing the consumption of plastic, an important part of the circular economy strategy. Its goal for reducing the negative impacts of this waste by 2030 involves the various economic sectors committing to taking care of their natural surroundings and meeting the following aims:

- Gradually substituting the materials used in single-use products.

- Strengthening the value chain.

- Promoting reusable products in stores.

- Guaranteeing environmental management in food delivery.

- Properly managing oxo-degradable and oxo-bio-degradable plastics.

- Guaranteeing the prohibition of entry and use of single-use plastics in Colombia's National Parks System.

CHAPTER 3

The environment, a cross-cutting prong of national development

As we have repeated many times throughout this book, true change with regards to the environment comes with transforming habits and the way we consume, with using technology to our advantage and with strengthening the idea that we can all contribute to avoiding a greater climactic disaster. Colombia's commitment to confronting this involves transforming production activities so that they are truly sustainable. For example, we must make progress in converting agricultural production so that it reduces its impact on ecosystems, and introducing better techniques and new technology for managing natural resources in the best manner. It is also imperative to drive sustainable activities through the development of new financial, economic and market instruments.

These objectives will help us to protect and improve our ecosystems, because the optimization of processes will allow us to properly manage environmental liabilities, guarantee better air and soil quality and care for our hydrological resources. Ultimately, all of these changes will improve public health, create new mechanisms which avoid inequality in access to resources and contribute to the goal of producing zero GHG emissions.

Conscious of the fact that this is vital to our development as a nation, throughout the national territory, and especially in strategic protection areas, cross-cutting projects have been developed with communities in order to create and implement production processes where biodiversity is a priority.

Environmental sustainability and green growth

Thanks to the Leticia Pact and international cooperation, the Amazon has witnessed the creation and strengthening of agro-environmental and sustained economic projects. In August 2020, almost a year after the signing of the agreement, around 20,000 farmers and indigenous people had benefitted from the development of environmental projects, including livestock conversion, the cultivation of rubber, cacao and non-timber products, governance and sustained economic growth plans, and plans aimed at women and families.

An example worth mentioning is that of a company dedicated to producing products for exportation using timber in the outskirts of Florencia, the capital of Caquetá, which is committed to the fight against deforestation, making use of around 90% of the timber during the production process. According to the entre-preneurs, this forest development project has involved local inhabitants, as it is economically viable, offering them an alternative to illicit crop growing or activities which contribute to the degradation of the ecosystems.

This company is a clear example of bioeconomy, an ever-more relevant term when discussing the real pos-sibility of transforming the world without affecting eco-nomic systems. Furthermore, this type of start-up shows us the route to a transition towards a sustainable econ-omy which incorporates circular economy concepts.

Another notable case is that of Hugo Parada and his family, who have decided to set aside 62 hectares of their farm for reforestation. "We have seen many positive changes: the fauna has increased, the flora has improved, and we know that we are doing something good for the environment", Parada says about his tree-planting project.

Elsewhere, the transformation of non-timber-yield-ing products has provided an alternative in the fight against deforestation. For example, in the Agrosolidaria plant in Florencia, around 250 families produce sweets, oils, chili sauces and cacao products, using a fruit known as sacha inchi or mountain peanut. "We control the entire chain, from production and transformation to commercialization, both with food products and cos-metics", explains the plant's director, Ricardo Calderón.

Similarly, the conversion of livestock rearing has been made possible thanks to the work of the Sinchi Institute, which has driven projects implementing garden centers for native species, halting the felling of trees and promoting a circular economy in around 11,800 hectares of protected areas (box 9).

Box 9. Progress in sustainable solutions and governance in the Amazon in 2021

1. 1,918,088 forest ordinance plans have been created and 48,642 hectares have been set aside for sustainable use as part of the *Visión Amazonía* program.
2. Indigenous communities will carry out four calls for proposals, one of which will exclusively be for projects run by women and families, with $13.236 million of resources to be allocated. These activities seek to strengthen indigenous communities' capacities for conserving the forests and carrying out sustainable production in their territories.

Equally, in the north-west of the country, communities in the Chocó department are looking to reduce the social and environmental impacts of artisanal and small-scale gold extraction. With a donation of 421,055 Euros, the United Nations Industrial Development Organization (UNIDO) and European Union's project, Empowering Chocó's Community Councils, seeks to give local inhabitants training on good environmental practices for responsible mining. It will also support the women of the communities in decision-making, strengthening their leadership capacities and giving them a decisive role in the sector.

This initiative, which will take place over 36 months from June 2021, seeks to improve the quality of life of the communities in Istmina and Medio Atrato, by teaching them about new tools and the transformation of natural resource management. It also supports community decisions, so that they can improve their means of local subsistence, fostering the development of economic activities which are in harmony with the ecosystems. It is hoped that, by 2022, an alternative business model will have been developed, that around 50 people (40% women) will have opted for alternative economic opportunities, and that a gold recovery team will have been set up.

ROYALTIES FOR THE COUNTRY'S ENVIRONMENTAL POLICY

In September 2020, Law 2056 came into force, marking a milestone in investment and project financing aimed at the protection and conservation of our strategic environmental areas, and in the fight against deforestation. For the first time in the country's history, a percentage of the resources from the General Royalties System were allocated to the implementation of environmental policies, specifically environmental sustainability, the protection of nature and the protection of the country's drainage basins (see figure 12).

FIGURE 12. BENEFITS OF ROYALTY ALLOCATION

 Local investment in the environment and sustainable development.

 The implementation of projects from the national strategy for the protection **of strategic environmental areas.**

 The creation and implementation of environmental management plans in protected areas or strategic ecosystems, formulated and adopted by the Regional Autonomous Corporations and the Sustainable Development Corporations in their respective jurisdictions, based on the guidelines provided by the Ministry of Environment and Sustainable Development and the National Planning Department.

 Investment in science, technology and environmental **innovation for sustainable development or non-conventional,** renewable energies which promote the energy transition and reduction of carbon emissions.

SOURCE: Prepared by the author

Of these resources, 1% (denominated the "environmental allocation"), plus 20% of certain taxes, is allocated to the conservation of strategic environmental areas and the national fight against deforestation. These resources will be allocated via calls for proposals by the Ministry of Environment and Sustainable Development and the National Planning Department, entities which define the criteria for each stage of the investment projects and offer spaces for the creation of consulting committees.

Furthermore, regulation law permits specific calls for proposals which benefit indigenous communities and groups, Afro-Colombian and black communities, communities from Palenque, and *Raizal* communities (from the three islands of San Andrés, Providencia and Santa Catalina), whose participation is vital to the transformation of production processes in the territories and the inclusion of ancestral wisdom on the conservation of ecosystems and sustainability.

And, as we believe in teamwork, these calls will be coordinated between the national government and the indigenous communities' decision-making entities, which include the Indigenous Guard and their associations, indigenous authorities and councils, associations of councils and other entities and organization structures registered with the Interior Ministry.

Nature-based solutions

One of the pillars of the "Produce while preserving, and preserve while producing" strategy is the creation of inclusive and innovative businesses, which depends, in large part, on the implementation of nature-based solutions and business solutions which guarantee a balance between production and the conservation of our biodiversity. In this sense, the protection and sustainable management of resources is vital to the construction of peace settings, which is why we are developing, across the country, different actions to protect our natural patrimony, alongside strategic actors like the local communities, biodiversity's guardians.

The positive results of this strategy can not only be seen in the national setting, but also in regional and international commercial promotion and business conferences. For example, the green business fair, Bioexpo, has been an important shop window for promoting the responsible production and consumption of goods and services based on agrodiversity, BioTrade, ecotourism and ethnotourism, among others. In July 2021, 2,581 green businesses had been verified, generating 30,661 jobs in the country. Of these, 613 are based in territories affected by the conflict.

Furthermore, apart from boosting the consumption of goods and services which guarantee the care for our ecosystems, green businesses are fundamental to the care of forests. Thirty-two percent of these are developing BioTrade production systems, that is to say systems that process products and services using natural resources, under environmental criteria.

An excellent example of this community development is the butterfly nursery. Recognized as a green business and a sustainable BioTrade alternative, the sustainable *Alas de Colombia* (Wings of Colombia) project has not only promoted the conservation of native plants and trees, it has also allowed 20 rural families – the majority of which are made up of female heads of households – to improve their quality of life and receive an income. According to its manager and co-founder, Vanessa Wilches Restrepo, "at *Alas de Colombia*, we have witnessed the cultural, social and environmental transformation that has developed around this sustainable production project. We are targeting the construction of a better country through opportunities in rural areas, which will also allow us to continue being the richest country in the world in terms of butterflies".

Similarly, responsible consumption also has positive effects. By promoting organic agricultural production, we can reduce the degradation of soil and restore hectares of ecosystems. Examples of this are the green businesses selling cacao, fruit trees, and vegetables whose production cycles have avoided the use of chemicals. According to the Ministry of Environment and Sustainable Development, 29% of the country's green businesses are dedicated to sustainable agricultural systems.

In the same vein, through the circular economy, reuse and recycling, we can stop tons of waste ending up in landfill sites or contaminating ecosystems as a result of poor management. Carbon dioxide emissions will also be reduced if we opt for alternative energy sources. In 2020, green businesses dedicated to making use of recycled waste collected 965 tons of materials. By stopping this waste from getting to landfill sites, the emission of the equivalent of 2,837 metric tons of carbon dioxide was avoided.

In terms of implementing ecotourism activities, Colombia has already seen positive results, both in the protection of forests and land conservation. By mid-

2021, 10,932 hectares had been protected thanks to ecotourism, food production based on native fruits and handicrafts using natural fibers.

Responsible consumption is a fundamental step towards protecting our forests, and if we do not learn to consume better, the road to sustainability will become blocked.

NATURE TOURISM AND START-UPS FOR THE AMAZON

The strengthening of communities is essential to the conservation of ecosystems. In the Amazon, for example, nature tourism in protected areas is a great source of income. That is why it is vital to develop good practices which allow locals to promote their economic activities with sustainability criteria. That is what the "Produce while preserving, and preserve while producing" strategy is about.

Currently, there are registered green businesses in the country offering guide services, ecotourism centers, tour operators and travel agencies, eco-activities and adventure tourism, accommodation, agro-tourism and gastronomy. This virtual portfolio promotes an environmentally-responsible tourism, fostering the development of businesses which care for our biodiversity. In the case of the Amazon, there are 96 green businesses focusing on nature tourism, which promote nature appreciation, leisure and recreational activities, cultural interaction, and sporting activities in natural settings (box 10).

Box 10. Green businesses in the country, and what goods and services they offer

1. **Guide services:** 90 businesses dedicated to hiking and sighting of flora and fauna.

2. **Ecotourism centers:** 79 businesses offering this service, including accommodation, food, guides and ecological activities.

3. **Tour operators and travel agencies:** 63 businesses offering packages to various destinations.

4. **Ecological activities and adventure tourism:** 50 businesses offering sporting, adventure, ethnotourism, cultural and well-being activities.

5. **Accommodation:** 40 businesses offering some form of accommodation with board.

6. **Agrotourism:** 30 businesses offering an agro-ecological experience with local communities.

7. **Gastronomy:** 2 businesses offering this service. They are restaurants and food and preserve vendors making up part of the tourist experience.

NOTE: the location of green businesses by region is as follows: Amazon (96), Caribbean (59), San Andrés, Providencia and Santa Catalina (27), Central Region (68), Antioquia – Coffee Triangle (34), Llanos and the Santanders (23), and Pacific (47).

SOURCE: MinAmbiente (2020q).

A FUEL MADE FROM COFFEE WASTE

In the Coffee Triangle, there is a push to generate renewable energy from coffee waste, coffee being the country's largest export. This start-up, verified as a green business, has allowed for the management of coffee residues in the agricultural areas where they are generated most, with the aim of converting them into biofuels.

Located in Pereira, the capital of Risaralda, this business converts waste from coffee and agricultural production into a biofuel alternative to replace the use of firewood, coal, coke, pellets and gas. This biofuel alternative reduces emissions of ash, CO_2 and sulfur, contributing to a reduction in GHG emissions. In the words of Juan Daniel García, owner of Garcabas, "we take [the waste] to the company, which is where the treatment, cleaning, classification, chopping, homogenization, compacting, mixing and everything else is done".

According to the Ministry of Agriculture, in 2020, 12.6 million bags of green coffee were registered for export. This represents 15% of the country's agricultural GDP, and is the source of income for 545,000 rural families, generating more than 2.5 million jobs, directly and indirectly.

GREEN BUSINESSES TO PROTECT LAKE TOTA

The basin of Lake Tota, which covers an area between the municipalities of Cuítiva, Tota, Aquitania and Sogamoso, in Boyacá, is one of Colombia's most important water sources. It is also vulnerable to the effects of climate change, not only because of the varied climate which affects high mountain ecosystems, but also because of the plentiful economic activity of agricultural production. Let us not forget that this area produces 80% of the spring onion consumed in the country.

Consequently, part of the work being carried out to protect Lake Tota is the implementation of food security projects and good practices in the production of spring onions and potatoes, as well as in livestock activities. Territorial management, adapting rainwater harvesting practices, participatory meteorological monitoring practices, ecological restoration, agroforestry germination practices, and sustainable tourism practices are vital to the creation of green businesses. These will help with the conservation of the lake's ecosystems and guarantee the social conditions and economic fabrics of rural families who make a living from agricultural production. It is estimated that this could benefit around 160 people, improving their relationship with their natural surroundings and guaranteeing sustainable management of natural resources.

Roughly 30% of green businesses are dedicated to organic and agroecological production, benefitting 4,819 farmers with indirect income, as partners of the green businesses, or with direct income, as employees of these production activities with a positive environmental impact. Furthermore, this model will contribute to the implementation of adaptation measures which benefit the agricultural sector and the community as a whole in Lake Tota.

However, this is just a part of the project which is being carried out to protect Lake Tota and reduce the negative effects of economic activity on its biodiversity. The project for the 'adaptation to the impacts of climate change on the Andes's water resources' (AICCA, for its Spanish acronym) is evaluating Lake Tota in order to identify climactic adaptation measures which could be replicated in other ecosystems. By better understanding the territories and creating nature-based solutions, Lake Tota's farming community can reap economic benefits while respecting the environment. And farmers in other departments can replicate this model of an eco-system-based production.

Environmental carers

It is proven that the greatest obstacle to environmental care practices is often the economy. That is why the "Payments for environmental services" program drives the sustainable management of natural resources and ecosystems and guarantees a source of income for the communities.

The program consists of an economic incentive, whether it be money or in kind, so that owners of plots and land located in strategic ecosystems can carry out actions to preserve and restore them. With these actions, communities contribute to slowing down the extraction of wood from forests, avoiding fires, creating watering troughs for livestock away from rivers, reducing the use of pesticides in crops and improving production practices so that their impact on ecosystems is reduced.

Through the Peace with Legality policy, the payments for environmental services program has guaranteed the sustainable management of 115,000 hectares, benefitting more than 6,500 families across the country. The goal is to cover 196,000 hectares under this conservation framework over the four-year period of 2018-2022.

Part of the strategy for meeting this goal is strengthening awareness on the ground of payments for environmental services, particularly in order to foster the design of local projects. The Ministry of Environment and Sustainable Development has already carried out more than 150 training sessions in territorial entities and with environmental authorities.

To date, there have been projects aimed at the conservation of ecosystems with high deforestation rates in the Caquetá, Guaviare, Meta and Antioquia departments. Territorially Focused Development Plans (PDET, for their Spanish acronym) have also been put in place in 13 municipalities, and results have been seen in 54 municipalities which are located in paramos, and 114 which contain forests. In 2021 alone, 58 projects in

municipalities with paramos and high levels of deforestation have been identified.

The goal for 2022 is to execute 9,500 natural conservation contracts, through which the rural population in
22 municipalities can become partners of the state, generate income and look after the ecosystems, by implementing projects in partnership with local environmental
and agricultural entities. The objective of these contracts
is to implement processes of voluntary substitution of
illicit crops in Forest Reserve areas.

INCENTIVES IN THE AMAZON

As part of the Leticia Pact, payments for environmental
services and conservation projects in the Amazon have
been promoted. In Caquetá alone, the goal is to conserve
3,000 hectares of forest, which will benefit more than
300 families.

According to the Ministry of Environment and
Sustainable Development's Environmental Territorial
Code, in the municipalities of Cartagena del Chairá,
Solano, Puerto Guzmán and Puerto Leguízamo, more
than 403 families are already benefitting from the conservation of approximately 35,187 hectares affected by
deforestation.

Guaviare is one of the departments where the results
have been most positive and payments for environmental services have generated opportunities for local development and poverty reduction while protecting strategic

ecosystems. In this department, the Amazon Forest Incentive (IFA, for its Spanish acronym) has guaranteed the commitment of 679 families in the municipalities of Calamar, San José del Guaviare, Miraflores and El Retorno, who contribute to the conservation of forests, with the aim of fighting against deforestation in an area of 18,680 hectares.

The goal of this incentive in Caquetá, Guaviare, Putumayo and southern Meta is to recruit 1,600 farming families in order to protect 100,000 hectares of forest with an investment of $1.516 million per year.

Additionally, it aims to recruit 600 jungle protection volunteer families, who will gain access to the Jungle School initiative's environmental education benefits.

As of September 30, 2021, there are 1,454 families benefitting from the general payments for environmental services blueprint, with a total of $588,000 contributing to the protection of 110,838 hectares.

THE CITIES ARE ALSO TAKING PART
Payments for environmental services have also been implemented in the cities, particularly in Bogotá, Cali, Popayán and Neiva. This program, which aims to conserve 85,000 hectares across the national territory, is of great interest to mayors' offices, as they can use incentives to promote the conservation of the ecosystems of strategic areas which provide environmental services and supply their aqueducts.

In 2020, Bogotá's local environment authority reported progress in its joint work with the Ministry of Environment, the objective of which is to consolidate a productive, inclusive, resilient and sustainable rural territory, based on responsible production frameworks. Payments for environmental services join the conservation plan for the Sumpaz paramo, with nearly 100 families in the Sumapaz, Usme, Ciudad Bolívar, Santa Fe and Chapinero localities contributing to the protection of 1,000 hectares, in order to counteract water contamination, deforestation and the excessive use of natural resources.

A sustainable future thanks to climate funding

Plans for adaptation to and mitigation of climate change need funding for their development, their implementation and for impact evaluation. For Colombia, it is vital to guarantee a flow of capital in order to achieve the long-term aim of consolidating a carbon neutral economy and reducing or avoiding the impact of climate change on ecosystems.

According to the OECD, climactic funding is necessary to promote low-carbon, climate-resilient development.

As maintained by the Permanent Finance Committee (PFC) of the United Nations Framework Convention on

Climate Change (UNFCCC), the availability of capital flows allows for a reduction in GHG emissions and vulnerability to the effects of climate change, and increases the resilience of various ecosystems.

As well as the mandates of the Paris Agreement (COP21, 2015) - which have demanded greater transparency and the development of monitoring mechanisms for climactic funding for the mitigation of GHG emissions and ensuring of climate resilience -, the SDGs have contributed to the definition of financial support indicators as part of goal 13 on climate action. That is why the purpose of target 13.a is so important. It relates to:

> Implementing the commitment undertaken by developed-country parties to the United Nations Framework Convention on Climate Change to a goal of mobilizing jointly $100 billion annually by 2020 from all sources to address the needs of developing countries in the context of meaningful mitigation actions and transparency on implementation and fully operationalize the Green Climate Fund through its capitalization as soon as possible (United Nations, 2015).

Colombia is a key actor in the Global South, as the fourth-largest receiver of climate funding in the region, according to the National Planning Department. But our country does not only receive financial support. In 2014, we committed to contributing 6 million dollars to the

Green Climate Fund, the financial mechanism of the UNFCCC for developing countries.

Furthermore, we are committed to consolidating spaces for the positioning and mobilization of climate funding in the region. The seven editions of the Climate Finances event, promoted by our country, have explored local and international experiences in order to create and share knowledge about risk management, climate entrepreneurship, the bioeconomy, nature-based solutions, among other actions and solutions which foster – jointly – economic reactivation and sustainable development.

It is precisely these actions and solutions which are connected to the design and structuring of Green Taxonomy, a novel classification system which allows for the identification of truly green investments and capital markets. Using a combination of concrete environmental definitions and objectives, we can determine which economic activities, assets, and public and private sector actors do not really contribute to the adaptation to and mitigation of climate change, the optimal management of land and water, the development of the circular economy, the prevention and control of contamination, and the conservation of our biodiversity.

So, in July 2021, the Ministry of Finance and Public Credit launched a reference framework for the future issuance of green bonds, which will allow for the covering of costs associated to a portfolio of 27 investment projects, up to a total of $526,000. This is an important decision by the government, given that we will have selection, evaluation and resource management principles, and a commitment to report to investors on projects associated to the issuance of green bonds included in the National General Budget (PGN, for its Spanish acronym).

The Minister of Finance and Public Credit, José Manuel Restrepo, has explained that the first allocation of green bonds will allow our country to fulfill its international commitments on good sustainable financing practices and guarantee a clear path to meeting our environmental goals: "It will offer clarity to investors interested in financing sustainable investment projects, which will not only contribute to diversifying our investor base, but also to reducing our impact on the environment, thanks to this new financing alternative".

Eligible projects need to meet certain performance indicators and contribute to the following categories: 1) management, use and sanitation of water; 2) clean transportation; 3) ecosystem services and protecting biodiversity; 4) non-conventional, renewable energy sources; 5) the circular economy, and 6) sustainable, climate change-adapted agricultural production.

The good news regarding transparency, responsibility and sustainable financing does not end with the issuance of green bonds. We are also pioneers in the creation of a MRV (monitoring, reporting and verification) system for climate funding, a methodology which allows us to estimate the climate funding in our country, and constantly improve the quality of the information and data. With that, we can guarantee an increase in the reliability of the system so that we can make comparisons over time.

As an overarching framework, we have a National Climate Change Policy (PNCC, for its Spanish acronym), which establishes our country's vision and governance framework. Its guidelines articulate all the decisions and strategies aimed at mitigating carbon emissions and promoting resilience to the impacts of climate change.

The following are Colombia's strategies for mitigating the effects of climate change:

- The Colombian Strategy for Low-Carbon Development.

- The National Plan for Adapting to Climate Change (PNACC, for its Spanish acronym).

- The strategy for the reduction of GHGs caused by deforestation and the degradation of forests, and for conservation and increased CO_2 captures (REDD+).

- The Public Finance Policy for Natural Disaster Risks.

- The National Strategy for Climate Funding (ENFC, for its Spanish acronym), which will be updated in 2022 with the support of the IDB and a joint effort with SISCLIMA's Finance Management Committee.

With the approval of Ruling 289 of February 2016, the National Climate Change System (SISCLIMA, for its Spanish acronym) was created in order to coordinate, bring together, formulate, follow and evaluate regional and national management of the adaptation to the effects of climate change and reduction of emissions. In particular, this project has sought to develop strategies which integrate the economic, social and particular needs of the territories, in order to create a balance between economic growth and the sustainable use of natural resources.

In order to reduce carbon emissions and become more resilient, we insist that we must ensure we have climate funding. Therefore, SISCLIMA's Finance Management Committee has focused on strengthening the National Strategy for Climate Funding (ENFC, for its Spanish acronym), based on the results of arbitrations on public spending in our country.

This is the first inter-institutional, public-private coordination mechanism centered on the capital flow to ensure a sustainable future. It is an integral part of the "planning instrument line of the PNCC's climate change management".

The purpose of this strategy is to ensure that our country is more competitive, thanks to sustainable economic development. The future lies in "achieving the transition towards a greener, more resilient, low-carbon economy" (Rudas et al., 2016, p.12). And this panorama is possible if robust funding mechanisms, which guarantee an investment in climate change and the conservation of natural resources, are established. That is to say that the national government commits to incorporating climate funding in the country's economic planning.

Financial resources do not just come from private companies and the financial sector. They also come from national public resources and international contributions. Together, the flow of resources can drive strategic mechanisms and actions in order to build a vision of the country based on climate financing and establishing what role each actor plays in the fight against climate change.

With regards the private sector, its contribution makes up 62% of total global investments in climate change (Rudas et al., 2016, p.17). In Colombia, the contribution of the financial sector in 2017 was $139 million on products with an environmental benefit. In 2014, the contribution of the production sector was $56 million in investments into the protection and conservation of the environment (Sebastian Lema et al., n.d., p.13). These figures will be updated in 2022, which will allow us to identify more precisely what resources are necessary in order to meet our climate change objectives.

In terms of mitigation funding, a total investment of $15 million is needed; that is around $1,679,000 a year (Sebastian Lema et al., n.d., p.12) if we are to meet our commitment to reduce GHG emissions by 51% by 2030. A fiscal space (public budgetary resources which have not been spent and which can be allocated to policies of interest) of \$526,000 a year in public finances has been identified, which could be effectively invested in meeting our climate change goals (Rudas et al., 2016, p.17). Furthermore, meeting this goal is dependent upon the provision of international support of 30%.

Funding for adaptation to climate change is a challenge, given that the goals are not quantified. In Colombia, we must define the actions necessary to guarantee adaptation and resilience that are in line with the needs of the territories (Sebastian Lema et al., n.d., p.11).

THE NATIONAL STRATEGY FOR CLIMATE FUNDING

As an instrument for supporting investment in climate change, Colombia has created a system for measuring climate funding, which is unique in terms of the precision of its results. The MRV (monitoring, reporting and verification) system was developed jointly by the National Planning Department, the World Resources Institute (WRI) and the Climate Finance Group of Latin America and the Caribbean (GFLAC, for its Spanish acronym), and is made up of the following:

- **Measuring:** the result of estimating allocated, received and mobilized financial resources for actions aimed at mitigation of and adaptation to climate change from various national and international public and private sources.

- **Reporting:** the result of presenting information on financial resources provided and mobilized, in terms of amounts, sources and destination, among others.

- **Verification:** the result of evaluating if the information on climate financing is correct and precise. This allows for the verification of the effectiveness and efficiency of climate funding.

The methodology does not only allow us to examine public climate spending, but also to make future projections of this funding and identify gaps and opportunities for more efficient resource management. The most important thing is that, based on its results, we can make decisions and recommend policies which ensure a sustainable and scalable capital flow in our country (DNP, 2021b).

Life's reflection

There were a number of reasons behind this book and, without doubt, the most important one was making a contribution to a carbon neutral Colombia which preserves its biodiversity and nature. As president, I have written more than 40 notebooks of my reflections on various topics and I have kept up my commitment to not letting a single day go by without writing about the government's work and the experiences which have enriched my life. This was perhaps driven by my personal habit of sleeping just five hours a day and seeking a thorough documentation of all of the topics which make up part of a task as demanding as governing Colombia.

As a country, we have a goal for this decade and the next 30 years. Our task should be to meet the sustainable development goals, ensure a reduction of 51% of our GHG emissions by 2030, have zero deforestation by the same year, making sure that 30% of our territory is within protected areas, and achieving carbon neutrality by 2050. These are perhaps the most ambitious objectives in our history, but we are on the right path, considering that we are leading the energy transition in Latin America and the Caribbean, and making large steps towards clean transportation, the circular economy, protecting areas, fighting against deforestation, and protecting the oceans and paramos.

But the biggest challenge to our national goals and, above all, our strategy, lies within each of our citizens. This strategy does not exclusively depend on the government, or the private sector, environmental organizations, academia or science. The success of this strategy depends on each one of us as individuals, on the way that we consume, on the way that we reduce our individual carbon footprint, on how we teach by example and at the same time demand and scrutinize the institutions' fulfillment of their duty.

The road to zero, the road to carbon neutrality, is our duty, our guiding light to overcoming the pessimistic view that development is naturally carbon intensive and is inevitably an enemy of well-being. Our goal is to prove that our growth will be clean, sustainable, in harmony with nature, and the embodiment of the very magic contained in our beautiful biodiversity.

Every page of this book is aimed at contributing to this great journey and showing that, together, we can do it. That is why setting off on the road to zero means building an agenda on life, and for life and, in that sense, this beautiful reflection from Gabriel García Márquez is more fitting than ever:

> *Neither floods nor plagues, nor famine nor cataclysms, nor even eternal war century after century have managed to reduce the tenacious advantage that life has over death.*

COP26: a road to leadership for Colombia

At the time of completion of this book, the COP26 summit in Glasgow has come to an end. Once again, heads of state came together to discuss and put forward our points of view on the measures we should take to deal with the climate crisis that is facing humanity.

I arrived in Glasgow accompanied by various people from my team. María Paula Correa, my Chief of Staff; the Environment Minister, Carlos Eduardo Correa, and the Minister for Mining and Energy, Diego Mesa, were just some of the main participants in Colombia's role in this historic meeting. I assigned them the responsibility of presenting all of the efforts we have made over more than three years to set an irreversible environmental agenda for our country. With the Colombian Ambassador in London, Antonio José Ardila, and the unwavering support of leaders including the United Kingdom's

Environment Minister, Zac Goldsmith, and the United Kingdom's Ambassador in Colombia, Colin Martin Reynolds, as well as the support of the Prime Minister of the United Kingdom, Boris Johnson and the Prince of Wales, our country contributed in a COP for the first time, taking an undisputed leading role.

It was three long days of intense and grueling work, but they were undoubtedly beneficial. Colombia showed the world how we have gone from an irrelevant 0.2% of non-conventional, renewable energies on our grid to 20%, made up of already-running projects, projects to be launched in the next eight months and projects awarded at the last auction, which places us as the leaders of this process in Latin America and the Caribbean. Similarly, Colombia shared with the world the road taken towards green hydrogen in our territory, and how Ecopetrol has become the first self-generator of non-conventional, renewable energy and the first company to order an electrolyzer for the production of hydrogen in 2022.

In the midst of COP26, Colombia also demonstrated a unique determination to protect forests. Alongside Prime Minister Johnson, and with a strategy that France's president, Emmanuel Macron, has also participated in, we encouraged a wide declaration on the protection of forests and biodiversity and, as a country, we committed to having 30% of our territory designated as a protected area by 2022. In order to prove this unique commitment, we used the opportunity of Glasgow to expand our protected marine areas by 160,000 km^2 – the largest declaration by a government on protected marine areas in Colombia. Alongside Panama, Costa Rica and Ecuador, we constitute the largest protected marine area on the planet.

Just as these actions validated Colombia's leadership role, so too did the demonstration of historic advancements, including: the Environmental Crimes Law, which harshens sanctions against deforestation; the Energy Transition Law, which offers incentives for the use of new sources of energy, including hydrogen; the commitment to plant 180 million trees by 2022; progress in clean transportation, consolidating Latin America's largest electric public transport and cargo fleet; and, shortly, the discussion and approval in Congress of the Climate Action Law, which will turn this whole process into a major state policy for reaching carbon neutrality by 2050 and reducing GHG emissions by 51% by 2030.

Colombia also joined other countries in driving immediate, impactful action to reduce methane emissions by 30% by 2030. Alongside US President Joe Biden, former Secretary of State, John Kerry (the US Special Presidential Envoy for Climate), President Moon of South Korea and the president of Argentina, Alberto Fernández, we spearheaded this declaration, which was joined by more than 90 countries and which, without doubt, will mark a milestone in collective action.

Furthermore, at COP26, we led dialogues on the fair market prices for coal credits and promoted the mobilization of resources to fund our joint strategy with the IDB, CAF (Development Bank of Latin America), World Bank, and the cooperation agencies of the United Kingdom, Germany, Norway, France, Sweden and the United States, placing special emphasis on creating effective funding and compensation mechanisms for achieving the greatest environmental investment in Colombia's history.

Over these three days, as a country we also joined the climate action transparency and traceability agenda, promoted by the OECD and its Secretary-General, Mathias Cormann, we extended our Amazon protection programs with the United Kingdom and we joined the Bezos Earth Fund agenda, which seeks to finance the conservation of strategic ecosystems.

The road to zero was the strategy we presented, which was lauded and which motivated the backing of public and private institutions, multilateral institutions and cooperation agencies, philanthropic organizations and international capital funds, which see in our country a coherent and consolidated agenda on the protection of our greatest riches: biodiversity.

The COP is a unique and special space for debate, reflection and collective construction. Boris Johnson's leadership has been fundamental, as has that of Zac Goldsmith, and Alok Sharma, President of the summit, in encouraging immediate action. There is a long way to go before all countries come to a conclusive agreement, but the reality is that there is no Planet B, we cannot rethink the goal of not surpassing 1.5 degrees centigrade, nor can we stop demanding that the world's largest and most powerful nations reduce their emissions by a minimum of 45% by 2030.

The challenges we face are enormous, the discussions and negotiations will continue, but something has been cemented in the minds of all those who attended COP 26: if a country like Colombia, which only contributes 0.6% of global GHG emissions, has set goals and met many of them, why can the nations who have contributed most to the climate crisis not follow this same path?

Our country cannot wait for others; we have the moral duty to act now, without delay. That is why we will not stop following the greatest environmental commitment in our history; for Colombia, COP 26 will always be a turning point, the moment we showed the world an agenda, a road to zero, the path to follow so that carbon neutrality is etched in the mind of every citizen.

DUBAI, NOVEMBER 5, 2021

Reviews

66 Now, more than ever, leadership matters in the world. We need bright lights to remind us of what matters and to urge us to action. *The Road to Zero* brings us President Duque's clear vision of the urgency of climate change and the imperative of building a better future - for ourselves and for our children. He outlines the available approaches and technologies that are within our grasp, and inspires us to build new cities, new economies, and new approaches to resource use and conservation - all the fundamentals to safeguarding the planet that is our home."

CARTER ROBERTS, PRESIDENT AND CEO
OF THE WORLD WILDLIFE FUND WWF

"We all need to be comfortable with zero – zero waste, zero extinctions, zero deforestation, zero emissions. In his landmark and brilliantly optimistic book, *The Road to Zero*, President Iván Duque lays out a compelling case of how one country, Colombia, despite the many challenges it is facing, is showing the way to carbon neutrality and positive nature conservation. *The Road to Zero* is an invitation to governments, communities, and the private sector to join in a shared journey – one that we cannot afford to sit out – towards a more shining, resilient future for our planet and our way of life. Every president in every country should be required to not only read this book, but also to write one of their own. Without such a roadmap we will never make meaningful progress and we are already woefully late."

DR. M. SANJAYAN, CEO CONSERVATION INTERNATIONAL

"There is no shortage of fine words on the environment from politicians around the world, but real action is rare. Here though, we have a bold and brilliant vision from the elected leader of one of the world's greatest countries; a global nature superpower. And President Duque's words have indeed been accompanied by action, and on an exhilarating scale. He is a true champion - of both Colombia's and the global environment.

In this urgent but wonderfully optimistic book, he shows us how the path to stability and prosperity involves reconciling our lives and economies with the natural world on which we all fundamentally depend."

LORD ZAC GOLDSMITH, MINISTER FOR THE PACIFIC
AND THE INTERNATIONAL ENVIRONMENT OF THE UK

"This book shows President Duque's determination and thought leadership in charting Colombia's ambitious pathway towards net zero emissions, putting the country at the forefront of the global fight against climate change. Spanning energy transitions, biodiversity and sustainability, *The Road to Zero* offers insights into the statecraft behind Colombia's leadership under President Duque on energy and environment issues in Latin America and beyond."

FATIH BIROL, EXECUTIVE DIRECTOR
INTERNATIONAL ENERGY AGENCY

"Colombia is a country of stunning beauty and biodiversity, home to every major ecosystem, from tropical coasts to alpine tundra, deserts, rainforests, and open savannas. President Iván Duque has long championed this

remarkable biodiversity and the wondrous cultural diversity of his country. In The Road to Zero he offers a roadmap for Colombia and for the world for protecting our natural and cultural heritage and for achieving sustainable development."
Jeffrey D. Sachs,

UNIVERSITY PROFESSOR AT COLUMBIA UNIVERSITY, PRESIDENT OF THE UN SUSTAINABLE DEVELOPMENT SOLUTIONS NETWORK

"President Duque is a global leader that has made the environment and sustainable development a priority. His experience and ambition led Colombia to adopt one of the most ambitious plans to tackle climate change, placing nature at the heart of the strategy to reduce emissions by 50% by 2030."

CHRISTIAN SAMPER, CEO WILDLIFE CONSERVATION SOCIETY

Bibliography

Bello, J. C., Báez, M., Gómez, M. F., Orrego, O., & Nägele, L. (2014). *Biodiversidad: Estado y tendencias de la biodiversidad continental de Colombia. Instituto Alexander von Humboldt.*

Bogotá Environment Ministry. (2020). *El Pago por Servicios Ambientales (PSA) es una herramienta efectiva para cuidar y proteger los ecosistemas. Secretaría de Ambiente de Bogotá.* http://www.ambientebogota.gov.co/c/journal/view_article_content?groupId=10157&articleId=9681876&version=1.2.

CIAT. (2018). *Productividad de la tierra y rendimiento del sector agropecuario medido a través de los indicadores de crecimiento verde en el marco de la Misión de Crecimiento Verde en Colombia. DNP.*

Departamento Administrativo Nacional de Estadística (DANE), & Ideam. (2015). *Hacia la construcción de la cuenta del agua a nivel nacional. https://www.dane.gov.co/files/investigaciones/pib/ambientales/PI-Hacia-la-construcci%C3%B3n-de-la-Cuenta-del-Agua-Nacional.pdf.*

Departamento Administrativo Nacional de Estadística (DANE). (2021). *Exports (EXPO)*. Technical Bulleting May 2021.

Departamento Nacional de Planeación (DNP). (2018). IV. Pacto por la sostenibilidad: producir conservando y conservar produciendo. In *Bases del plan nacional de desarrollo 2018-2022 "Pacto por Colombia Pacto por La Equidad"* (*pp. 459–520). DNP.

Departamento Nacional de Planeación (DNP). (2021a). ¿Qué es el financiamiento climático? Finanzas del Clima. https://finanzasdelclima.dnp.gov.co/FinanzasColombia/Paginas/Que-es.aspx.

Departamento Nacional de Planeación (DNP). (2021b). ¿Qué es el financiamiento climático? Portal MRV de Financiamiento Climático. https://mrv.dnp.gov.co/MRV/Paginas/Que-esel-financiamiento-climático.aspx.

Departamento Nacional de Planeación Planeación & SISCLIMA. (2020b). *VII Evento Finanzas del Clima 2020*. *https://finanzasdelclima.dnp.gov.co/Documents/Memorias Evento Finanzas del Clima 2020.pdf*

Departamento Nacional de Planeación, & SISCLIMA. (2020a). *Memorias del VII Evento Finanzas del Clima 2020. VII Evento Finanzas Del Clima 2020. https://finanzasdelclima.dnp.gov. co/Paginas/DNP-invita-a-inscribirse-en-VII-EventoFinanzas-del-Clima-2020.aspx*.

DNP, PNUMA, & GGGI. (2017). *Evaluación del Potencial de Crecimiento Verde para Colombia*. DNP, Fedesarrollo, GGGI, PNUMA.

198

DNP. (2018). *CONPES 3943 Document.* DNP.

González, J., Cubillo, M., Arias, A., Chadid, M., Joubert, F., & Cabrera, E. (2016). *Caracterización de las principales causas y agentes de deforestación a nivel nacional periodo 2005-2015.* IDEAM, MADS, ONU-REDD.

IDEAM. (2018). *Resultados del monitoreo de la deforestación 2017.* IDEAM.

Invemar. (2018). *Informe del estado de los ambientes marinos y costeros 2017.*

Investor Relations Colombia, Ministry of Housing and Public Credit. (2021). Bulletin n°. 38 *Colombia lanza marco de referencia y prepara primera emisión de bonos verdes soberanos.* https://www.irc.gov.co/webcenter/portal/ IRCEs/ pages_Deuda/bonosverdes.

Lema, S., Barreneche, J. C., Sabogal, J., Quintero, C., Franco, J. F., Bohórquez, V., Cruz, E., Pulido, P., Peñuela, L., Avendaño, J., Pinzón, J., Rueda, L., Camacho, J., & Restrepo, P. (n.d.). *Estrategia Nacional de Financiamiento Climático.* DNP.

Ministry of Environment and Sustainable Development, N.-. (2021a). *"¡Es un hecho histórico para el país!": Ministro de Ambiente tras aprobación del proyecto de ley que penaliza la deforestación* [Press release]. https:// www.minambiente.gov.co/index.php/noticias/5160-es-unhecho-historico-para-el-pais-ministro-de-ambientetras-aprobacion-del-proyecto-de-ley-que-penaliza-deforestacion.

Ministry of Environment and Sustainable Development. (2016). *Sistema Nacional de Cambio Climático – SISCLIMA.*

Asuntos Ambientales y Sectorial y Urbana - Articles. https:// www.minambiente.gov.co/index.php/temas-asuntosam bientales-y-sectorial-y-urbana/10-asuntos-ambientales-y-sectorial-y-urbana-articulos/302-sistema-nacional-de-cambio-climatico-sisclima.

Ministry of Environment and Sustainable Development. (2017). *Arranca Proyecto GEF-BID para la consolidación del Sistema Nacional de Áreas Protegidas* [Press release]. https:// www.minambiente.gov. co/index.php/ noticias-minambiente/3156-arranca-proyecto-gefbid-para-la-con solidacion-del-sistema-nacional-deareas-protegidas.

Ministry of Environment and Sustainable Development. (2018). *Logros ambientales fueron definitivos para acceso de Colombia a la OCDE* [Press release]. https://www. minambiente.gov.co/index.php/ noticias-minambi ente/3898-logros-ambientales-fueron-definitivos-para-acceso-de-colombia-a-la-ocde.

Ministry of Environment and Sustainable Development. (2019a). *Bioexpo realizará la primera rueda de negocios verdes internacional en el Valle del Cauca* [Press release]. https://www.minambiente.gov.co/index.php/noticias-minambiente/4493-bioexpo-realizara-la-primera-rueda-de-negocios-verdes-internacional-en-el-valle-del-cauca.

Ministry of Environment and Sustainable Development. (2019b). *Colombia, el segundo país más biodiverso del mundo, celebra el Día Mundial de la Biodiversidad* [Press release]. https://www.minambiente.gov.co/index.php/ noticias-minambiente/4317-colombia-el-segundo-pais-mas-biodiverso-del-mundo-celebra-el-dia-mundial-de-la-biodiversidad.

Ministry of Environment and Sustainable Development. (2019c). *Colombia preside negociaciones en favor de la capa de ozono en 31a Reunión de las Partes del Protocolo de Montreal en Roma* [Press release]. https://www.minambiente.gov.co/index.php/noticiasminambiente/4524-colombia-preside-negociacionesen-favor-de-la-capa-de-ozono-en-31a-reunion-de-laspartes-del-protocolo-de-montreal-en-roma.

Ministry of Environment and Sustainable Development. (2019d). *Colombia ratificó tratado global contra el mercurio* [Press release]. https://www. minambiente.gov.co/index.php/noticias-minambiente/4417-colombia-ratifico-tratado-global-contra-elmercurio.

Ministry of Environment and Sustainable Development. (2019e). *Congreso aprueba ley que ratifica la Enmienda de Kigali* [Press release]. https://www.minambiente.gov.co/index.php/noticias-minambiente/4335-congreso-aprueba-ley-que-ratifica-la-enmiendade-kigali.

Ministry of Environment and Sustainable Development. (2019f). *En la Cumbre por la Amazonía, se firmó el "Pacto de Leticia", un acuerdo que establece enfrentar muchas de las causas de la deforestación* [Press release]. https://www.minambiente.gov.co/index.php/noticiasminambiente/4448-en-la-cumbre-por-la-amazonia-sefirmo-el-pacto-de-leticia-un-acuerdo-que-estableceenfrentar-muchas-de-las-causas-de-la-deforestacion.

Ministry of Environment and Sustainable Development. (2019g). *'Hoy tenemos que levantar nuestra voz a nivel presidencial y hacer este Pacto, donde todos coordinemos nuestras acciones para proteger la Amazonía': Presidente Duque* [Press release]. https://www.minambiente.gov.co/index. php/noticias-minambiente/4418-hoytenemos-que-levantar-nuestra-voz-a-nivel-presidencialy-hacer-este-pacto-donde-todos-coordinemos-nuestrasacciones-para-proteger-la-amazonia-presidente-duque.

Ministry of Environment and Sustainable Development. (2019h). *MinAmbiente ha logrado gestionar más de 158 millones de dólares de cooperación internacional para la protección de nuestros recursos naturales* [Press release]. https://www.minambiente.gov.co/index.php/ noticias-minambiente/4535-minambiente-ha-logradogestionar-mas-de-158-millones-de-dolares-de-coopera cion-internacional-para-la-proteccion-de-nuestrosre-cursos-naturales.

Ministry of Environment and Sustainable Development. (2019i). *Países firmantes del Pacto de Leticia por la Amazonía presentaron Plan de Acción para su implementación* [Press release]. https://www.minambiente.gov.co/index.php/ noticias-minambiente/ 4580-pacto-amazonia-plan-accion-colombia.

Ministry of Environment and Sustainable Development. (2019j). *Páramos de Colombia, fábricas de agua y cunas de biodiversidad. Ministerio de Ambiente y Desarrollo Sostenible*

[Press release]. https://www.minambiente.gov.co/index. php/noticias-minambiente/4714- paramos-de-colom bia-fabricas-de-agua-y-cunas-de-biodiversidad.

Ministry of Environment and Sustainable Development. (2019k). *Persecución conjunta de aserradores ilegales y biopiratas, una de las tareas inmediatas del Plan de Acción del Pacto de Leticia por la Amazonía. Ministerio de Ambiente y Desarrollo Sostenible* [Press release]. https://www. minambiente.gov.co/index.php/noticiasminambiente/ 4583-persecucion-conjunta-de-aserradores-ilegales-y-biopiratas-una-de-las-tareas-inmediatasdel-plan-de-accion-del-pacto-de-leticia-por-laamazonia.

Ministry of Environment and Sustainable Development. (2020a). *139.100 hectáreas de tierra con alta oferta de servicios ecosistémicos son protegidas en Caquetá. Ministerio de Ambiente y Desarrollo Sostenible* [Press release]. https:// www.minambiente.gov.co/index.php/ noticias-minam biente/4890-139-100-hectareas-de-tierra-con-alta-oferta-de-servicios-ecosistemicos-son-protegidas-en-caqueta.

Ministry of Environment and Sustainable Development. (2020b). *Colombia eliminará al año 2021, la producción de aislantes térmicos que agotan la capa de ozono* [Press release]. https://www.minambiente.gov. co/index.php/ noticias-minambiente/4811-colombiaeliminara-al-ano-2021-la-produccion-de-aislantes-termicos-que-agotan-la-capa-de-ozono.

Ministry of Environment and Sustainable Development.

(2020c). *Colombia prepara la actualización de sus compromisos de acción climática* [Press release]. https://www. minambiente.gov.co/index.php/ noticias-minambiente/ 4770-colombia-prepara-laactualizacion-de-sus-compro misos-de-accion-climatica.

Ministry of Environment and Sustainable Development. (2020d). *Con siembra de palma de cera, Minambiente realizó recorrido por Páramo Las Tinajas* [Press release]. https:// www.minambiente.gov. co/index.php/noticias-minambiente/4860-con-siembra-depalma-de-cera-mi-nambiente-realizo-recorrido-porparamo-las-tinajas.

Ministry of Environment and Sustainable Development. (2020e). *Desde Leticia, SINA fortalece la protección de la Amazonía Colombiana* [Press release]. https://www. minambiente.gov.co/index.php/noticiasminambiente/ 4894-desde-leticia-sina-fortalece-la-proteccion-de-la-amazonia-colombiana.

Ministry of Environment and Sustainable Development. (2020f). *Despliegue del SINA en la Amazonía deja grandes resultados* [Press release]. https://www. minambiente.gov. co/index.php/noticias-minambiente/4898-despliegue-del-sina-en-la-amazonia-deja-grandesresultados.

Ministry of Environment and Sustainable Development. (2020g). *Empresas con sostenibilidad ecológica, una apuesta para la Amazonía.* [Press release]. https://www.minambi-ente.gov.co/index.php/ noticias-minambiente/4893-em presas-con-sostenibilidad-ecologica-una-apuesta-para-la-amazonia.

Ministry of Environment and Sustainable Development. (2020h). *En Guaviare, 66 familias recibieron el Incentivo Forestal Amazónico para avanzar en la lucha contra la deforestación.* [Press release]. https://www. minambiente.gov.co/index.php/noticias-minam biente/4888-en-guaviare-66-familias-recibieron-el-incentivo-forestal-amazonico-para-avanzar-en-la-lucha-contra-la-deforestacion.

Ministry of Environment and Sustainable Development. (2020i). *Gobierno Nacional prohíbe la pesca artesanal e industrial de tiburón en el país* [Press release]. https://www. minambiente.gov.co/index.php/ noticias/4876-gobierno-nacional-prohibe-la-pesca-artesanal-e-industrial-de-tiburon-en-el-pais.

Ministry of Environment and Sustainable Development. (2020j). *Gobierno Nacional radica proyecto de ley contra la explotación ilícita de minerales* [Press release]. https://www. minambiente.gov.co/index.php/ noticias-minambiente/ 4762-gobierno-nacional-radicaproyecto-de-ley-contra-la-explotacion-ilicita-deminerales.

Ministry of Environment and Sustainable Development. (2020k). *Gran alianza para transformar a Leticia en una biodiverciudad* [Press release]. https://www.minambiente.gov. co/index.php/noticias-minambiente/4886-gran-alianza-para-transformar-a-leticia-en-una-biodiverciudad.

Ministry of Environment and Sustainable Development. (2020l). *Herencia Colombia, una realidad* [Press release]. https://www.minambiente.gov.co/index.php/noticias-minambiente/4798-herenciacolombia-una-realidad.

Ministry of Environment and Sustainable Development. (2020m). *Lagos de Tarapoto, ejemplo de restauración ecológica* [Press release]. https://www. minambiente.gov. co/index.php/noticias-minambiente/ 4892-lagos-de-tara poto-ejemplo-de-restauracionecologica.

Ministry of Environment and Sustainable Development. (2020n). *Más de 1.500 millones de pesos serán destinados a proyectos sostenibles del Valle del Cauca* [Press release]. https://www.minambiente.gov. co/index.php/noti-cias-minambiente/4861-mas-del-500-millones-de-pe-sos-seran-destinados-a-proyectossostenibles-del-valle-del-cauca.

Ministry of Environment and Sustainable Development. (2020o). *Más de 20.000 familias indígenas beneficiadas con proyectos agroambientales y de economía sostenible en la Amazonía* [Press release]. https:// www.minambiente.gov. co/index.php/noticiasminambiente/4772-mas-de-20-000-familias-indigenasbeneficiadas-con-proyectos-agro ambientales-y-de-economia-sostenible-en-la-amazonia.

Ministry of Environment and Sustainable Development. (2020p). *Más de 22 mil millones de pesos serán destinados para proteger nuestros páramos* [Press release]. https:// www.minambiente.gov.co/index.php/ noticias-minam biente/4840-mas-de-22-mil-millones-de-pesos-seran-destinados-para-proteger-nuestrosparamos.

Ministry of Environment and Sustainable Development. (2020q). *MinAmbiente lanzó el portafolio de turismo de*

naturaleza en la Amazonía [Press release]. https://www.
minambiente.gov.co/index.php/ noticias-minambiente/
4885-minambiente-lanzo-elportafolio-de-turismo-de-
naturaleza-en-la-amazonia.

Ministry of Environment and Sustainable Development.
(2020r). *Minambiente y Asocapitales promueven estrategia
de Pagos por Servicios Ambientales en ciudades capitales del
país* [Press release]. https:// www.minambiente.gov.co/
index.php/noticiasminambiente/4775-minambiente-
y-asocapitales-promueven-estrategia-de-pagos-por-ser-
vicios-ambientalesen-ciudades-capitales-del-pais.

Ministry of Environment and Sustainable Development.
(2020s). *Ministerio de Ambiente destina 15 millones de
dólares para invertir en 16 páramos de Colombia* [Press
release]. https://www.minambiente.gov. co/index.php/
noticias-minambiente/4901-ministeriode-ambiente-des
tina-15-millones-de-dolares-parainvertir-en-16-paramos-
de-colombia.

Ministry of Environment and Sustainable Development.
(2020t). *Ministro Ricardo Lozano presentó estrategia colombiana de Economía Circular en Davos* [Press release]. https://
www.minambiente.gov.co/ index.php/noticias-
minambiente/4606-estrategiacolombiana-de-economia-
circular-en-davos.

Ministry of Environment and Sustainable Development.
(2020u). *Negocio verde de Pereira produce biocombustible
con residuos de café* [Press release]. https://www.minam-

biente.gov.co/index.php/noticiasminambiente/4743-ne gocio-verde-de-pereira-producebiocombustible-con-resi duos-de-cafe.

Ministry of Environment and Sustainable Development. (2020v). *Presidente Iván Duque sancionó la primera Ley de Regalías que destina recursos para fortalecer el Sistema Nacional Ambiental* [Press release]. https://www.minambiente.gov.co/index.php/ noticias-minambiente/4825-presidente-ivan-duquesanciono-la-primera-ley-de-rega lias-que-destina-recursos-para-fortalecer-el-sistema-nacional-ambiental.

Ministry of Environment and Sustainable Development. (2020w). *Sector Ambiente, beneficiario de recursos por Sistema General de Regalías.* [Press release]. https://www.minambiente.gov.co/index.php/ noticias-minambiente/4807-sector-ambiente-beneficiario-de-recursos-por-sistema-general-de-regalias.

Ministry of Environment and Sustainable Development. (2020x). *Sector floricultor le apuesta a la economía circular* [Press release]. https://www.minambiente.gov.co/index.php/noticias-minambiente/4906- sector-floricultor-le-apuesta-a-la-economia-circular.

Ministry of Environment and Sustainable Development. (2020y). *Un llamado a la acción global por la protección de los páramos* [Press release]. https://www.minambiente.gov.co/index.php/noticiasminambiente/4819-un-llamado-a-la-accion-globalpor-la-proteccion-de-los-paramos.

Ministry of Environment and Sustainable Development. (2020z). *Universidades y Centros de Investigación se unen a la Estrategia Nacional de Economía Circular* [Press release]. https://www.minambiente.gov.co/index.php/noticias-minambiente/4779- universidades-y-centros-de-investigacion-se-unen-a-laestrategia-nacional-de-economia-circular.

Ministry of Environment and Sustainable Development. (2021). *Portafolio de Negocios Verdes. Sistema de Información Ambiental de Colombia - SIAC.* https://negocios-verdes-mads.hub.arcgis.com/.

Ministry of Environment and Sustainable Development. (2021aa). *Los recicladores, claves para la economía circular: Ministro de Ambiente.* [Press release]. https://www.minambiente.gov.co/index.php/ noticias-minambiente/4983-los-recicladores-claveseconomia-circular-ministro.

Ministry of Environment and Sustainable Development. (2021ab). *Más de 115.000 hectáreas de ecosistemas están siendo conservadas gracias a los Pagos por Servicios Ambientales* [Press release]. https:// www.minambiente. gov.co/index.php/noticiasminambiente/5137-mas-de-115000-hectareas-de-ecosistemas-estan-siendo-conservadas-gracias-a-lospagos-por-servicios-ambientales.

Ministry of Environment and Sustainable Development. (2021ac). *Minambiente aporta para una refrigeración más amable en los hogares de los colombianos* [Press release]. https://www.minambiente. gov.co/index.php/ noticias-minambiente/5173- minambiente-aporta-para-una-refrigeracion-masamable-en-los-hogares-de-los-colombianos.

Ministry of Environment and Sustainable Development. (2021ad). *Minambiente avanza en agenda bilateral con países de la Unión Europea* [Press release]. https://www.minambiente.gov.co/index.php/ noticias-minambiente/ 4984-minambiente-avanza-enagenda-bilateral-con-pai ses-de-la-union-europea.

Ministry of Environment and Sustainable Development. (2021ae). *Minambiente lanza el programa 'Vigías Forestales Contra Incendios' en Providencia* [Press release]. https://www.minambiente.gov.co/index.php/ noticias-min ambiente/4958-minambiente-lanza-el-programa-vigias-forestales-contra-incendios-en-providencia.

Ministry of Environment and Sustainable Development. (2021af). *Minambiente y Bomberos Indígenas, de la mano para reducir incendios forestales* [Press release]. https://www.minambiente.gov.co/index.php/ noticias-min ambiente/5186-minambiente-y-bomberosindigenas-de-la-mano-para-reducir-incendios-forestales.

Ministry of Environment and Sustainable Development. (2021ag). *MinAmbiente y DNP anuncian paso crucial para evitar y controlar la deforestación en el país* [Press release]. https://www.minambiente. gov.co/index.php/noticias-minambiente/4922- minambiente-y-dnp-anuncian-pa-so-crucial-para-evitar-y-controlar-la-deforestacion-en-el-pais.

Ministry of Environment and Sustainable Development.

(2021ah). *Minambiente y DNP diseñaron una metodología que beneficia a hogares rurales* [Press release]. https://www. minambiente.gov.co/index.php/ noticias-minambiente/ 5044-minambiente-y-dnp-disenaron-una-metodologia-que-beneficia-a-hogares-rurales.

Ministry of Environment and Sustainable Development. (2021ai). *Ministerio de Ambiente entrega incentivo económico a familias de Tierralta por conservar bosques* [Press release]. https://www.minambiente.gov. co/index.php/ noticias-minambiente/4962-ministeriode-ambiente-en-trega-incentivo-economico-a-familiasde-tierralta-por-conservar-bosque.

Ministry of Environment and Sustainable Development. (2021aj). *Ministro Correa presentó el modelo de biodiverci-udades en la Asamblea del BID* [Press release]. https://www. minambiente.gov.co/index.php/ noticias-minambiente/ 5000-ministro-correa-presentoel-modelo-de-biodiver-ciudades-en-la-asamblea-del-bid.

Ministry of Environment and Sustainable Development. (2021ak). *Negocios verdes, aliados en la protección de los bosques* [Press release]. https://www.minam biente.gov.co/index.php/noticias-minambiente/5167-negocios-verdes-aliados-en-la-proteccion-de-los-bos ques.

Ministry of Environment and Sustainable Development. (2021al). *Operación Cangrejo Negro: avanza en la recuper-ación de San Andrés, Providencia y Santa Catalina* [Press release]. https://www.minambiente.gov.co/index.php/

noticias-minambiente/5031- operacion-cangrejo-ne-gro-avanza-en-la-recuperacionde-san-andres-providen-cia-y-santa-catalina.

Ministry of Environment and Sustainable Development. (2021am). *Páramo de Santurbán: las 3 acciones que el Ministerio ejecuta tras incendio* [Press release]. https://www.minambiente.gov.co/index.php/ noticias-minambiente/4985-paramo-de-santurban-las3-acciones-que-el-ministerio-ejecuta-tras-incendio.

Ministry of Environment and Sustainable Development. (2021an). *Presidente Duque pidió unir esfuerzos para salvar el planeta y generar conciencia* [Press release]. https://www.minambiente.gov.co/index.php/ noticias-minambiente/5053-presidente-duque-pidio-unir-esfuerzos-para-salvar-el-planeta-y-generarconciencia.

Ministry of Environment and Sustainable Development. (2021ao). *Presidente Duque presenta la iniciativa Biodiverciudades en el Foro Económico Mundial* [Press release]. https://www.minambiente.gov. co/index.php/ noticias-minambiente/4941-presidenteduque-presenta-la-iniciativa-biodiverciudades-enel-foro-economico-mundial.

Ministry of Environment and Sustainable Development. (2021ap). *Presidente Duque y ministro Correa lanzaron el ambicioso programa Un Millón de Corales por Colombia* [Press release]. https://www.minambiente.gov.co/index. php/noticias/5158-presidente-duquey-ministro-correa-lanzaron-ambicioso-programa-unmillon-de-corales.

Ministry of Environment and Sustainable Development. (2021aq). *Proyecto de adaptación al cambio climático en el Lago de Tota ha beneficiado a más de seis mil habitantes* [Press release]. https://www.minambiente.gov.co/index. php/noticias-minambiente/5126- proyecto-de-adap tacion-al-cambio-climatico-en-el-lagode-tota-ha-bene-ficiado-a-mas-de-seis-mil-habitantes.

Ministry of Environment and Sustainable Development. (2021ar). *Proyecto de cooperación internacional ha apoyado la declaratoria de protección de más de seis millones de hectáreas* [Press release]. https://www.minambiente.gov. co/index.php/noticias-minambiente/5157-proyectode-cooperacion-internacional-ha-apoyado-la-declaratoria-de-proteccion-de-mas-de-6-millones-de-hectareas.

Ministry of Environment and Sustainable Development. (2021as). *Red de viverismo comunitario: un proyecto que fortalece la paz y los bosques en la Amazonía* [Press release]. https://www.minambiente. gov.co/index.php/noticias-minambiente/5177-red-deviverismo-comuni-tario-un-proyecto-que-fortalece-lapaz-y-los-bosques.

Ministry of Environment and Sustainable Development. (2021at). *Se iniciará proyecto que beneficiará a 4000 familias rurales en zonas de frontera forestal* [Press release]. https://www.minambiente. gov.co/index.php/noticias-minambiente/5148-seiniciara-proyecto-que-be neficiara-a-4000-familiasrurales-en-zonas-de-fronteras.

Ministry of Environment and Sustainable Development. (2021au). *"Se necesita una acción climática urgente y ambi-*

ciosa": ministro Correa en diálogo del Wilson Center [Press release]. https://www.minambiente.gov.co/index.php/noticias-minambiente/5032-senecesita-una-accion-climatica-urgente-y-ambiciosaministro-correa-en-dialogo-del-wilson-center.

Ministry of Environment and Sustainable Development. (2021av). *Se puede hacer conservación junto a las comunidades que habitan en los páramos: Ministerio de Ambiente* [Press release]. https://www.minambiente.gov.co/index.php/noticias-minambiente/5120- se-puede-hacer-con servacion-junto-a-las-comunidades-que-habitan-en-los-paramos-ministerio-deambiente.

Ministry of Environment and Sustainable Development. (2021b). *Acciones ambientales para la paz: una prioridad del Gobierno Nacional* [Press release]. https://www.minambiente.gov.co/index.php/noticiasminambiente/5206-acciones-ambientales-para-la-pazuna-prioridad-de-gobierno-nacional.

Ministry of Environment and Sustainable Development. (2021c). *Acciones que conservan sanos nuestros bosques, los pulmones de todos* [Press release]. https://www.minambiente.gov.co/index.php/noticiasminambiente/5009-acciones-que-conservan-sanosnuestros-bosques-los-pulmones-de-todos.

Ministry of Environment and Sustainable Development. (2021d). *Alianza renovada entre Colombia, Alemania, Noruega y el Reino Unido sobre cooperación en bosques y clima* [Press release]. https://www.

minambiente.gov.co/index.php/noticias-minambiente/
5001-alianza-renovada-entre-colombia-alemania-no
ruega-yel-reino-unido-sobre-cooperacion-en-bosques-y-
clima.

Ministry of Environment and Sustainable Development.
(2021e). *Amazonía, una prioridad para Minambiente* [Press
release]. https://www. minambiente.gov.co/index.php/
noticias-minambiente/ 4998-amazonia-una-prioridad-
para-minambiente.

Ministry of Environment and Sustainable Development.
(2021f). *Cambio climático, a tenerse en cuenta en obras de
infraestructura* [Press release]. https://www.minambiente.
gov.co/index.php/noticiasminambiente/4974-cambio-cli
matico-a-tenerse-encuenta-en-obras-de-infraestructura.

Ministry of Environment and Sustainable Development.
(2021g). *Colombia, el país de las mariposas* [Press release].
https://www.minambiente.gov. co/index.php/
noticias-minambiente/5172-colombia-elpais-de-las-ma
riposas.

Ministry of Environment and Sustainable Development.
(2021h). *Colombia cuenta con un plan nacional para la
gestión sostenible de los plásticos de un solo uso* [Press
release]. https://www.minambiente. gov.co/index.php/
noticias-minambiente/5125-colombia-con-un-plan-na-
cional-para-la-gestion-sostenible-de-los-plasticos-de-
un-solo-uso.

Ministry of Environment and Sustainable Development.
(2021i). *Colombia inicia acciones para la gestión sostenible*

de la biomasa residual [Press release]. https://www.min-ambiente.gov.co/index.php/noticiasminambiente/5170-colombia-inicia-acciones-para-lagestion-sostenible-de-la-biomasa-residual.

Ministry of Environment and Sustainable Development. (2021j). *Colombia le cierra el cerco al tráfico ilegal de especies silvestres* [Press release]. https:// www.minambiente. gov.co/index.php/noticias-minambiente/5124-colombia-le-cierra-el-cerco-al-trafico-ilegal-de-especies-silvestres.

Ministry of Environment and Sustainable Development. (2021k). *Compra de bolsas plásticas en puntos de venta se redujo cerca de un 70 % en Colombia: Minambiente* [Press release]. https://www.minambiente.gov.co/index.php/noticias-minambiente/5185- compra-de-bolsas-plasti-cas-en-puntos-de-ventas-seredujo-cerca-de-un-70-por-ciento-en-colombia.

Ministry of Environment and Sustainable Development. (2021l). *Con apoyo internacional, Colombia lanza proyecto para recuperar y conservar la Ciénaga Grande de Santa Marta* [Press release]. https://www. minambiente.gov.co/index.php/noticias-minambiente/ 5134- con-apoyo-internacional-colombia-lanza-proyec-to-pararecuperar-y-conservar-la-cienaga-grande-de-san-ta-marta.

Ministry of Environment and Sustainable Development. (2021m). *Con gobernanza forestal, el Minambiente le apunta a la conservación y al uso sostenible de los bosques* [Press release]. https://www. minambiente.gov.co/index.php/

noticias-minambiente/5168-con-gobernanza-forestal-el-ambiente-le-apuntaa-la-conservacion-y-al-uso-sos-tenible-de-los-bosques.

Ministry of Environment and Sustainable Development. (2021n). *Continúa formación en economía circular: ahora 880 jóvenes y adultos más se capacitan en todo el país* [Press release]. https://www.minambiente.gov.co/index.php/ noticias-minambiente/5095- continua-formacion-en-economia-circular-ahora-880- jovenes-adultos-se-capacitan-en-todo-el-pais.

Ministry of Environment and Sustainable Development. (2021o). *De recorrido por Cundinamarca, el viceministro Galarza visitó proyectos de educación ambiental* [Press release]. https://www.minambiente.gov. co/index.php/ noticias-minambiente/5042-de-recorridopor-cundina-marca-viceministro-galarza-visito-proyectos-educacion-ambiental.

Ministry of Environment and Sustainable Development. (2021p). *Disminuye en un 30 % la deforestación en Meta, Caquetá y Guaviare durante primer trimestre de 2021* [Press release]. https://www.minambiente.gov. co/index.php/ noticias-minambiente/5189-disminuye-enun-30-por-ciento-la-deforestacion-en-el-meta-caquetay-guaviare-durante-primer-trimestre-del-ano.

Ministry of Environment and Sustainable Development. (2021q). *El 31 de marzo vence plazo para presentar planes de gestión ambiental de envases y empaques* [Press release]. https://www.minambiente. gov.co/index.php/

noticias/5015-31-marzo-vence-plazopara-presentar-planes-gestion-ambiental.

Ministry of Environment and Sustainable Development. (2021r). *El Minambiente acompaña un proyecto que empodera a comunidades del Chocó* [Press release]. https://www.minambiente.gov.co/index.php/noticias-minambiente/5176-el-minambiente-acompanaun-proyecto-que-empodera-a-comunidades-del-choco.

Ministry of Environment and Sustainable Development. (2021s). *En 16 ciudades se identificaron 48 iniciativas que reducirían 3,5 millones de toneladas de CO2 al 2030* [Press release]. https://www.minambiente.gov.co/index.php/noticias-minambiente/5112- en-16-ciudades-se-identificaron-48-iniciativas-quereducirian-3-5-millones-de-toneladas-de-co2-al-ano.

Ministry of Environment and Sustainable Development. (2021t). *En el Día de los Bosques Tropicales, el Minambiente cuenta cómo lucha Colombia contra la deforestación* [Press release]. https://www.minambiente.gov.co/index.php/noticias-minambiente/5164-enel-dia-de-los-bosques-tropicales-el-minambientecuenta-como-lucha-colombia-contra-la-deforestacion.

Ministry of Environment and Sustainable Development. (2021u). *Gobierno anunció nuevas iniciativas para la restauración ecológica de Providencia y Santa Catalina* [Press release]. https://www.minambiente.gov.co/index.php/noticias-minambiente/4930- gobierno-anuncio-nuevas-iniciativas-para-la-restauracion-ecologica-de-providencia-y-santa-catalina.

Ministry of Environment and Sustainable Development. (2021v). *Gobierno Nacional, con la lupa puesta en la deforestación* [Press release]. https://www. minambiente. gov.co/index.php/noticias-minambiente/ 5047-gobierno-nacional-con-la-lupa-puesta-en-la-deforestacion.

Ministry of Environment and Sustainable Development. (2021w). *Guía de Minambiente les permitirá a las ciudades saber cuántos gases emiten* [Press release]. https://www. minambiente.gov.co/index.php/noticias-minambiente/ 4996-guia-de-minambiente-lespermitira-a-las-ciudades-saber-cuantos-gases-emiten.

Ministry of Environment and Sustainable Development. (2021x). *Inversión social será clave para combatir la deforestación en el país en 2021* [Press release]. https://www. minambiente.gov.co/index.php/ noticias-minambiente/ 4923-inversion-social-seraclave-para-combatir-la-deforestacion-en-el-pais-en-2021.

Ministry of Environment and Sustainable Development. (2021y). *La iniciativa Biodiverciudades sigue avanzando para conectar a las ciudades colombianas con su biodiversidad* [Press release]. https://www. minambiente.gov.co/ index.php/noticias-minambiente/5106-la-iniciativa-biodiverciudades-sigue-avanzando-para-conectar-a-las-ciudades-colombianas-consu-biodiversidad.

Ministry of Environment and Sustainable Development. (2021z). *Los países de la Amazonía ya tienen un Protocolo para el Manejo de Incendios Forestales* [Press release].

219

https://www.minambiente.gov. co/index.php/noticias-minambiente/5069-los-paisesde-la-amazonia-ya-tienen-protocolo-para-el-manejode-incendios-forestales.

Ministry of Environment and Sustainable Development. (n.d.). *Nace Herencia Colombia: el programa para proteger nuestro capital natural para siempre* [Press release]. https://www.minambiente.gov. co/index.php/noticias-minambiente/3454-nace-herenciacolombia-el-programa-para-proteger-nuestro-capitalnatural-para-siempre.

Ministry of Agriculture. (2020). *Cosecha cafetera de 2020 cerraría con un valor de $9 billones, superior en 20% a 2019 y una de las más altas en 20 años* [Press release]. https:// www. minagricultura.gov.co/noticias/Paginas/Cosechacafetera-2020.aspx.

Ministry of Defense. (2021). *Logros de la política de defensa y seguridad.* https://www.mindefensa.gov.co/irj/go/km/ docs/Mindefensa/Documentos/descargas/estudios_sec-toriales/info_estadistica/Logros_Sector_Defensa.pdf.

Ministry of Housing and Public Credit. (2021). *Taxonomía Verde de Colombia - Fase I.* https://www.minhacienda. gov. co/webcenter/portal/TaxonomiaVerdeColombia/ pages_ taxonomiavercolombia.

Presidency of the Republic of Colombia. (2020). *El Gobierno Nacional prohíbe la pesca artesanal e industrial de tiburón en Colombia* [Press release]. https://idm. presidencia.gov. co/prensa/el-gobierno-nacional-prohibela-pesca-arte-sanal-e-industrial-de-tiburon-201126.

Presidency of the Republic of Colombia. (2021a). *En Cumbre mundial de Líderes, presidente Duque propone tres acciones para enfrentar el cambio climático* [Press release]. https://idm.presidencia.gov.co/prensa/en-cumbremundial-de-lideres-presidente-duque-propone-tresacciones-para-en-210422.

Presidency of the Republic of Colombia. (2021b). *Intervención del presidente Iván Duque Márquez en la Cumbre de Líderes sobre el Clima.* [Press release]. https://idm.presidencia.gov.co/prensa/intervencion-del-presidente-ivanduque-marquez-en-la-cumbre-de-lideres-sobr-210422.

Resolution no. 1342 of 24 December, 2020, which modifies Resolution 1407 of 2018. (2020) https://www.minambiente.gov.co/images/normativa/app/resoluciones/e8-Res_1342_de_2020_Modifica_la_res_1407_ de_2018.pdf.

Rudas, G., Rodríguez, O., Latorre, C., Osorio, J., Lacoste, M., & Camacho, J. (2016). *Marco para la Estrategia Colombiana de Financiamiento Climático. Econometría.*

Sistema de Información Ambiental de Colombia (SIAC). (2021). *Gases de Efecto Invernadero, GEI.* http://www.siac.gov.co/climaticogei.

United Nations. (2015). *Goal 13: Take urgent action to combat climate change and its impacts. Sustainable Development Goals.* https://www.un.org/sustainabledevelopment/climate-change/.

World Bank. (2021). *Urban population (% of total population) - Colombia. The World Bank Data. https://datos.bancomundial.org/indicador/SP.URB.TOTL.IN. ZS?locations=CO.*

San Andrés, Wildlife coral refuge

San Andrés, Wildlife coral refuge

San Andrés, Wildlife coral refuge

Vetas, Santander, view of the Santurbán paramo

Guaviare, view of the
La Lindosa valley

Vetas, Santander, view of the Santurbán paramo

Vetas, Santander, view of the Santurbán paramo

Vetas, Santander, view of the Santurbán paramo

Guayabero River, Colombian Orinoco region

Guayabero River, Colombian Orinoco region

Leticia, Colombia, Pre-COP15 Biodiversity, 2021

Leticia, Colombia, Pre-COP15 Biodiversity, 2021

Pétalo de Córdoba solar farm

Sumapaz National Natural Park

Visit and talks on the fight against deforestation in the Amazon

Serranía de Chiribiquete National Natural Park

Mavecure mountains, Puerto Inírida, Guainía

Guayabero River, Colombian Orinoco region

Nuquí, Chocó

Puerto Carreño, Vichada

Sumapaz paramo

Sumapaz paramo

Sumapaz paramo

The Amazon. Photo taken during the Amazon Celebration Week

El Paso solar farm,
Cesar

Electric transportation strategy

El Paso solar farm, Cesar

Electric transportation strategy

El Paso solar farm, Cesar

Speaking at COP26, Glasgow, United Kingdom

Declaration of the largest protected marine area in the world at COP26, Glasgow, United Kingdom. Iván Duque, President of Colombia; Guillermo Lasso, President of Ecuador; Laurentino Cortizo, President of Panama; and Carlos Alvarado, President of Costa Rica.

Chiribiquete mountains, Amazon region. Carlos Correa, Environment Minister; Iván Duque, President of Colombia; Francisco Cruz, Deputy Minister of Environmental Policies and Normalization; and Orlando Molano, head of the National Parks Authority.